The Fourth Secularisation

This book examines recent forms of secularisation to demonstrate that we are now witnessing a "fourth secularisation": the autonomy of lifestyles. After introducing two initial secularising movements, from *mythos* to *Logos* and from *Logos* to Christianity, the book sets out how from Max Weber onwards a third movement emerged that practised the autonomy of science. More recently, daily life radicalises Weber's secularisation and its scope has spread out to include autonomy of individual practices, which has given rise to this fourth iteration.

The book outlines these first three forms of secularisation and then analyses the fourth secularisation in depth, identifying its three main dimensions: the de-institutionalisation of the religious lifestyle; the individualisation of faith; and the development of new social forms in the religious field. These areas of religious practice are shown to be multiplying partly as a result of the general aestheticization of society. Individuals, therefore, aspire to personal styles of life with regard to beliefs and the choice of their own religious practices.

This book will be of great use to scholars of religious studies, secularisation and the sociology of religion.

Luigi Berzano is Emeritus Professor of Sociology at the University of Turin and tenured Professor of Sociology of Communication at the Salesian Rebaudengo University of Turin, Italy. He is co-editor of the *Annual Review of the Sociology of Religion*, and he directs the series *Spiritualità senza Dio?* (Spirituality without God?).

Routledge Focus on Religion

Amoris Laetitia and the Spirit of Vatican II
The Source of Controversy
Mariusz Biliniewicz

Muslim and Jew
Origins, Growth, Resentment
Aaron W. Hughes

The Bible and Digital Millennials
David G. Ford, Joshua L. Mann and Peter M. Phillips

The Fourth Secularisation
Autonomy of Individual Lifestyles
Luigi Berzano

For more information about this series, please visit: www.routledge.com/series/RFR

The Fourth Secularisation
Autonomy of Individual Lifestyles

Luigi Berzano

**Translated from the Italian
by Eunan Sheridan**

LONDON AND NEW YORK

First published in English 2019
by Routledge
2 Park Square, Milton Park, Abingdon, Oxon OX14 4RN

and by Routledge
605 Third Avenue, New York, NY 10017

First issued in paperback 2021

Routledge is an imprint of the Taylor & Francis Group, an informa business

© 2019 Luigi Berzano

Translated from the Italian by Eunan Sheridan

The right of Luigi Berzano to be identified as author of this work has been asserted by him in accordance with sections 77 and 78 of the Copyright, Designs and Patents Act 1988.

All rights reserved. No part of this book may be reprinted or reproduced or utilised in any form or by any electronic, mechanical, or other means, now known or hereafter invented, including photocopying and recording, or in any information storage or retrieval system, without permission in writing from the publishers.

Trademark notice: Product or corporate names may be trademarks or registered trademarks, and are used only for identification and explanation without intent to infringe.

Published in Italian by Mimesis Edizioni 2017

British Library Cataloguing-in-Publication Data
A catalogue record for this book is available from the British Library

Library of Congress Cataloging-in-Publication Data
A catalog record for this book has been requested

ISBN 13: 978-0-367-78802-5 (pbk)
ISBN 13: 978-0-367-26068-2 (hbk)

Typeset in Times New Roman
by Apex CoVantage, LLC

Contents

Acknowledgements — vii

Introduction — 1

1 From a single style to multiple styles — 6
   Definition of lifestyles 7
   The aestheticization of society 10

2 Spiritual revolution: Multiplication of forms — 18
   Spiritual individualisation 20
   Revolution of rising spiritual expectations 23
   Multiple spiritual identities 25
   Conclusion 26

3 The fourth secularisation — 30
   From mythos *to* Logos *31*
   From Logos *to Christianity 35*
   *Theological rupture: the divine is no longer cosmic
      order but a person 35*
   Ethical rupture: all individuals are equal 36
   *Spiritual rupture: a doctrine of salvation and of
      living a good life 37*
   Modernity and scientific autonomy 39
   Autonomy of lifestyles 41
   The drivers of the fourth secularisation 45
   Conclusion 54

4 Sense of religion in the secular age 62
Post-secular *versus* secular 63
Leaving (behind) the heteronomy of the religious 64
The religious beyond the secular 67
Structure of the religious in the future 70

Index 76

Acknowledgements

This volume, *The Fourth Secularisation: Autonomy of Individual Lifestyles*, is the conclusion of a research itinerary undertaken in the past few years and already explored in other publications, notably the book I published with Carlo Genova, *Lifestyles and Subcultures: History and a New Perspective*, Routledge, Abingdon-New York, 2015. I would like to take this opportunity to thank the people involved in the production of the present work: my university colleague Carlo Genova, with whom I have over the years shared reflections on styles of life; Mimesis, which has already published extracts from the text; Eunan Sheridan for the translation and June Anne Nuevo for the editing.

Introduction

"As Chartres, seen from afar, is just a cathedral, the village of Saint-Joachim is only a church; our countryside is strewn with naves and bell-towers which dominate it and reveal the location of communities . . ." (Le Bras, 1979: 9 [our translation]). Thus opens *L'église et le village*, the finest work by Gabriel Le Bras, who goes on to say that only when one follows the village paths do the clusters of houses appear, the alleyways and workplaces, the inhabitants, the social classes with their forms of life, work, feast-days and collective struggles. This is the image of the traditional Christian world which for centuries reflected the European countries with their rural parishes. Once, the religious landscape was structured as follows: the church and its belfry stood in the middle of the town, defining ecclesiastical territory, the stability of religious identity and the regular practice of the community faithful.

For decades now, two major transformations have been modifying this traditional European scenario: secularisation and religious pluralism. The former differentiates between the sacred and the profane, the spiritual and the religious, and introduces new means of recognition and legitimation; the latter injects into traditional European religions all the historical traditions of the Orient, new religious movements and, lastly, a growing presence of the Muslim world. The general effect is that which in sociology is usually called – with a metaphor derived from economics – "the religious market".

Today there is no area of economic, social, cultural or religious life which is not at the heart of a complex – both individual and collective – evolution. It is to this complexity that some of the foremost interpreters of present-day society (among others, Bauman, Beck, Giddens and Dahrendorf) refer when they identify its distinctive characteristics as "freedom", "choice", "uncertainty", "risk" and "fluidity". A specific trait of these social contexts, indeed, is the weakening of "vertical" processes of reproduction, those by means of which cultural models are transmitted from one generation to the next.

At the same time, we are witnessing increasing complexity of the organizational models *within* such environments. Consequently, individual attitudes and behaviour depend less and less upon one's position in the social structure and more and more upon one's personal elaboration of the resources and models made available by single biographical itineraries. This leads not only to an enlargement of the possibilities of choice offered to individuals but also to an impairment of the points of reference useful for guiding their choices. The result is a "horizontal society" and "horizontal lifestyles" in a landscape where identities and affiliations are ever-less ascribed and ever-more dependent upon individuals' spontaneous initiatives, thereby becoming more problematic and more reflexive (Berzano and Genova, 2010).

Chapter 1 refers to the topicality of lifestyles understood as the modalities according to which individuals organize their existence. Lifestyles are the profiles through which individuals communicate – to themselves and to others – who they are, to whom they feel similar and from whom they wish to distinguish themselves, defining a unitary sense of their living and behaving. Lifestyles belong to today's society, where individuals' behaviour is often no longer explicable by means of values, ideologies or even social status but rather by personal tastes, sensibility and interests – and fashion. These factors enjoy an importance today which was unthinkable in traditional societies where there was limited possibility of choice and options because life was custom and routine. We may say of lifestyles as we do of clothes, for example, that they are relational elements, the changing of a social body interacting with others: elements defining the individual's "profile", such as dress, home and surroundings. They are the moveable surface of social space, leaving traces along the way in the knowledge that living means leaving traces. Pointing out these fluid social elements does not imply denying the influence which various economic and structural processes continue to exercise upon the individual; the intention is rather to underline the complexity increasingly characterizing such processes. And this begs the question: What social bonds, what social forms, what models of action will develop – are indeed already developing – within contexts which have these characteristics?

Chapter 2 deals with religious identities and their respective lifestyles. Religions, churches and religious individuals themselves in their practices and beliefs are not exempt from the evolution described above. All research into contemporary religious phenomena agrees that in advanced modernity the various axiological systems are not cancelled but are rather increasingly perceived as a matter of free choice. The influence of economic transformations and of the great religious traditions continues to exercise its power over the individual, but with less effect. Ronald Inglehart's decades-long research

Introduction 3

documents the slow "silent revolution" whereby morality is stripped of many prohibitions and reduced to its essential core of respect for others; religion is stripped of all concepts which cannot be interpreted symbolically; politics is stripped of everything which does not respect the dignity of the citizen and the law appropriates the utopia of prevention, demoting dissuasion and repression (Inglehart, 1990, 1997; Norris and Inglehart, 2004). They are processes which, referring to the (general, uncertain) notion of "the dignity of the person", lead to greater individual freedom and autonomy (Stolz, 2016).

What bonds, social forms and lifestyles will develop within future religions? Will horizontal lifestyles weaken traditional forms of church affiliation based on the "vertical" reproduction of religious identities, beliefs and practices? Will forms of belonging chosen by individuals spread further? And will these affiliations really become weaker, problematic and reflexive? Will Georg Simmel's prediction that society based on *a style of life* will with modernity evolve into society founded upon *multiple lifestyles* be applicable also to religion (Pace, 2018)?

In more general terms, Chapter 3 defines the present form of the autonomy of religious lifestyles as "the fourth secularisation". In recent decades the secularisation theme has aroused great interest among scholars of both social sciences and the humanities. Lately the theme has enjoyed a revival stimulated by the opposition between those who see a return of the sacred and those who attribute lasting heuristic validity to the theory of secularisation, albeit divided into different declensions (Gorski and Altinordu, 2008; Norris and Inglehart, 2004). The present tome tends towards the latter interpretation. After the secularisation from Greek mythology to Classical philosophy, after the secularisation from the abstract *Logos* to Christianity, and after the third secularisation of science at the dawn of the modern age, the fourth – current – one will be the secularisation of individual lifestyles. The autonomy of science, claimed by Max Weber's secularisation, has extended also to the autonomy of individual practices "from the cradle to the grave". The range of individual needs and expectations today demands that they become more and more a range of publicly recognized rights. The secularisation of lifestyles implies that they depend decreasingly upon one's religion of belonging and increasingly upon individual choice. In this process of personalisation and stylistic self-awareness, spiritualities and religious individuals without a fixed religious status proliferate (Altglas, 2014). This does not foretell the death of the religious person but rather the individual's tendency to build one's own religious life project. Mass societies, therefore, fuel not only the "grey conformity" mentioned by some commentators but also individual differences. In the religious field too, new spiritual profiles take shape, attracting because of their free nature and their personalised horizontal practices, giving rise to composite, eclectic lifestyles chosen by

4 *Introduction*

the individual. The practices of which these latter mainly consist are based on interpersonal relations with other religious environments and individuals: these individuals may never meet in person but may communicate virtually through media and social networks. Everybody becomes a direct spectator of what is happening elsewhere. And it is these conditions of life which also weaken religious practices and behaviour acquired by birth. As a general rule, these lifestyles represent a religion composed of people who have chosen it on the basis of their needs, interests and personal sensibility. Everything contributes to emphasizing the typical nature of the styles, the differentiation even in individuals' lives.

Chapter 4 analyses religious forms in the *secular* context, the epoch considered by some as *abandoning religion's heteronomy*. It will attempt to answer Marcel Gauchet's question as to what will happen when "the Gods abandon the world and religions cease to signify their otherness, [and] it is the world itself which begins to seem the other . . . ?" (Gauchet, 1992: 297 [our translation]).

This Gauchet passage is an effective rendering of what I mean by the *secular* age, an epoch which – by some combination of circumstances – is witnessing on the terrain of secularisation new cultural and spiritual phenomena because of connections between the secularised world and religion. The *secular* age is not subsequent to secularisation but accompanies it and is an effect of it. The various secularisations have not emptied religion of its religious experiences but have transformed its connections with the diversity of the secularised world (De Groot, 2017). And it is in this phase, concomitant with the secularisation process, that a part of the traditional sacred is changed into more experiential forms, individualised, independent of defined dogmatic content and the confines of historical religions. The *secular* sacred is the set of new spiritual frames of mind of the *sacred* as distinct from the *profane* as well as the behaviour and social forms which express it.

References

Altglas V. (2014), *From Yoga to Kabbalah: Religious Exoticism and the Logics of Bricolage*, Oxford University Press, Oxford.
Berzano L., Genova C. (2010), *La società delle pratiche orizzontali. Percorsi di ricerca e ipotesi*, EMIL, Bologna.
De Groot K. (2017), *The Liquidation of the Church*, Routledge, Abingdon and New York.
Gauchet M. (1985), *Le désenchantement du monde. Une histoire politique de la religion*, Gallimard, Paris (It. Trans. *Il disincanto del mondo: una storia politica della religione*, Einaudi, Torino, 1992; Eng. Trans. *The Disenchantment of the World: A Political History of Religion*, Princeton University Press, Princeton, NJ, 1997).

Gorski P. S., Altinordu A. (2008), "After Secularization?", *Annual Review of Sociology*, XXXIV: 55–85.
Inglehart R. (1990), *Culture Shift in Advanced Industrial Society*, Princeton University Press, Princeton (It. Trans. *Valori e cultura politica nella società industriale*, ed. R. Cartocci, Utet, Torino, 1997).
Inglehart R. (1997), *Modernization and Postmodernization: Cultural, Economic, and Political Change in 43 Societies*, Princeton University Press, Princeton (It. Trans. *La società postmoderna: mutamento, valori e ideologie in 43 paesi*, Editori Riuniti, Roma, 1998).
Le Bras G. (1976), *L'église et le village*, Flammarion, Paris (It. Trans. *La chiesa e il villaggio*, Boringhieri, Torino, 1979).
Norris P., Inglehart R. (2004), *Sacred and Secular: Religion and Politics Worldwide*, Cambridge University Press, Cambridge.
Pace E. (2018), *Cristianesimo Extra-Large: La fede come spettacolo di massa*, EDB, Bologna.
Stolz J. et al. (2016), *(Un)beleiving in Modern Society: Religion, Spirituality, and Religious-secular Competition*, Routledge, Abingdon.

1 From a single style to multiple styles

Lifestyles have by now entered the language and interpretative models of social sciences, especially when researching the condition of youth and consumption. The apparently clear concept is in fact multidisciplinary, used by economics, sociology, psychology and anthropology. When it is applied to the analysis of individual or collective behaviour, it includes various fields related to projects, aspirations, consumption, behaviour and identity-building. The concept of lifestyles is particularly useful here in understanding religious-type forms of participation, belief and identity-building. The interest is in seeing whether such forms may indicate spiritual experiences and feelings, transform everyday (profane) time into festive (sacred) time, slow down the erosion of institutional bonds with historical religions and/or counteract the process of dissipation of religious systems into simple systems with secular meanings.

Georg Simmel (Simmel, 1890, 1896–7, 1900, 1908) is the scholar who has made the greatest contribution to the construction of a science of lifestyles. He it was who elaborated on the relationship between extension of social circles and the development of styles and identities; and who pointed out that styles of life have the double function of forming and characterizing a group, cementing its unitarity *ab intra* and differentiating it *ad extra* from other social groups.

It is the function of levelling and typifying, as well as individualising, so that the more differentiated the structure becomes the more the formal psychic qualities of the individuals who grow within it stand out. Norbert Elias makes the same point: "Individuality and social conditioning are not two different functions of men in their specific relationship. They express the individual's specific activity in relations with others. . . . In short, they express the *function of coin* and the *function of currency*" (Elias, 1990: 75–76 [our translation]).

From this Simmel concludes that whereas traditional society was characterized by a (single) *style of life*, modern society is characterized by (plural) *styles of life.* Many allude to this conclusion of Simmel's when, speaking of the present, they say, "No rules, only choices". This is the particular condition of the contemporary individual with unlimited power of access to styles among which s/he may choose according to one's tastes. In Simmel's view, the formation of a market of styles available to the individual – and the consequent decline of the style at the market level – is compensated for by the stylisation of the interiority with which individuals endeavour to express their subjectivity (Frisby, 1985: 65 ff.). Simmel believes the emblematic figure of this context is the metropolitan individual who, in addition to the fragmentation of lifestyles, experiences the disorienting overexcitement of fashions and consumption.

Definition of lifestyles

The definition offered here is based on the affirmation that contemporary societies are characterized by classes and groups with no fixed status, where the links between style of life and economic position are loosening and where lifestyles are increasingly founded upon personal choices.

In the setting-up of lifestyles – including religious lifestyles, as we shall see – we can observe various factors deriving from both the choices of each individual and the context in which s/he lives (the typology presented in Giddens, 1991). First, in advanced modernity the individual has to choose among multiple options; sometimes, when traditional options have disappeared, the individual must invent her/his own. Second, in an environment of greater uncertainty lifestyles multiply. The methodical doubt of contemporary societies assigns conditional trust to everybody, whether individuals or institutions, "until further notice". Abstract systems such as money, which penetrate daily life so deeply, normally offer multiple possibilities rather than pre-determined guidelines or precise recipes for action. Third, today's individual lives in a context of "pluralisation of the worlds of life", multiple segmented, differentiated environments. Lifestyles are expressions, and sometimes consequences, of the several settings or places where the individual lives.[1] Mass media also influence the plurality of choice and lifestyles. Electronic media in particular alter the "situational geography" of social life, continually producing new common elements and new differences. Lastly, attention paid to "tailoring" a lifestyle, involving all ages and environments (including the religious), implies the positive dimension of effort, risk and personal participation while it presents the critical dimension of assembly. There are biographical phases, such as adolescence and early adulthood, when the choice of a distinctive lifestyle enables one to indicate one's IN group as opposed to groups which are OUT. And the interpretation of lifestyles as rites of passage is confirmed by the example of women who, as soon as they find out that they are pregnant, adopt a style of life – clothes, diet, time management, attitudes – suited to their new condition.

As a result, the possibilities of using lifestyles as indicators of social classes and stratification, or of consumption, are limited in the present context where lifestyles are communicative and identity expressions ascribable to the individual's cultural and axiological system (Bourdieu, 1979, 1980, 1987, 2004; Bourdieu, Passeron, 1970). We therefore define a lifestyle as a social form including "a set of practices, with unitary and relational meaning, which is a distinctive model shared within a collectivity, without having either a pre-existent cognitive-axiological system or a pre-determined socio-structural condition as generative elements, even though it may be influenced by them" (Berzano and Genova, 2015: 177).

Let us now examine the elements of the definition individually (Berzano and Genova, 2015, Chapter 9). A lifestyle is a "social form" in Simmel's sense, a "form of association", a "formal mode of reciprocal attitude among individuals", a model type of reciprocal action, "forms characterizing groups of people united to live side-by-side, either one for the others or one with the others" (Simmel, 1896–97: 72. See also pp. 71–109).

We can therefore talk about a lifestyle as a configuration of reciprocal actions shared by a number of individuals – in the single clusters of shared individual practices which may be observed.

A social form does not perforce mean processes of direct interaction among people co-present in space and time. Even in the few cases where an individual carries out practices autonomously, it is still possible to talk about a lifestyle.

"Practice" means "a social activity considered in the way it is habitually carried out by an individual or a group" (Ansart, 1999: 416). *Habitually* is the operative word, distinguishing "practice" from Weber's "social action" (1922, Vol I: 4).

Practices suggest actions characterized by repetitiveness of varying frequency. Even when they do not derive from an explicit reflective process, they depend on individual choice and are therefore endowed with meaning for the actor. The concept is thus different from the traditional all-inclusive practice/theory opposition. Jedlowski (2003: 178) claims that "practice" is used vaguely, but the term suggests (in contrast with "action") the ideas of routine, habit (*habitus*), even tradition (cf. Bourdieu).

Parallel values, attitudes and sensibilities within a lifestyle may help in its interpretation. They are auxiliary elements, neither necessary nor sufficient unto themselves: a lifestyle may be unconnected with these three specific components; but if they are present while a framework of practices is absent, it is not a lifestyle.

The distinction between "sense" (the individual's interpretation of the set of practices making up the lifestyle as a whole) and "meaning" (the individual's interpretation of each lifestyle component) is precisely observed in this model.

The central point of interpretation-understanding is the intersection between the processes of comprehension (analysis of meaning, "direct observational understanding", identification of the *what*) and explanation (analysis of sense, "explanatory understanding", identification of the *why*). But whereas the comprehension process is essentially relevant to a simple sign-meaning connection, the explanation process complicates the analysis of the connection by inserting it into the framework of a broader interpretative context (i.e. a sense), thereby enriching meaning, its clarification and extension, by an action of contextualisation.

Lifestyle-analysis will therefore reconstruct the meaning attributed to individual practices, attempting to answer this question: "What does that practice mean to the actor?" It will also reconstruct the sense attributed to the complete set of practices: "Why are those practices adopted as a whole?" The meaning of each practice is influenced by every other relevant practice: a lifestyle's sense is unitary in that it is a form of organic action where single practices acquire meaning because they are interpreted in reciprocal interaction. The multiple practices may be read through the same interpretative model insofar as each practice is in reciprocal relations with the others: it can acquire full meaning only within this framework. The meaning is relational because it can only be reconstructed on the basis of the semantic insertion of a single practice among the others and their relationship with it; the consequent reconstruction of the meaning of each one will be possible only through the reconstruction of the overall framework of practices and its sense.

The profile of shared practices is not always identical for individuals referring to a lifestyle: it is a model, perhaps an "ideal type", based on a selection among shared practices and interpretative models, re-unified and intensified (Weber, 2011: 89 ff.) An individual may adopt only some of the lifestyle's practices, for which very reason s/he will (reciprocally) perceive his/her relationship with a model to which others are related.

Hypothetically there may be no "core" of practices shared by all those referring to a lifestyle: sharing is partial and different for each pair or subset of individuals. Mathematically, rather than being a list of circle-sets with a common superimposition area, a lifestyle may be seen as the intersection of circle-sets with (at least in pairs) some common area but without transversally shared areas.

Here the concept of generative element refers to those factors and processes which may constitute necessary and sufficient, logical and temporal, antecedents to the development of an individual's practices. However, when one speaks of a lifestyle, neither the cognitive-axiological framework nor the socio-structural conditions may be considered as the lifestyle's generative factors.

This does not mean that values and representations, or resources, bonds and socialisation processes, cannot influence an individual's lifestyle involvement: all these factors are relevant to the correct interpretation of that influence. For a framework of practices to be a lifestyle their adoption must not be generated by the effects exercised upon the individual's action by these factors.

What factors and contexts have favoured the multiplication of styles? We shall indicate five of the principal ones: *the aestheticization of society*; *cities and metropolises*; *reference groups*; *"loisirs"*; and *consumption*.

The aestheticization of society

Contemporary society, sometimes known as the *aesthetic society*, has discovered the fascination of lifestyles. Each individual is seeking her/his own style which will represent him/her, differentiate her/him from others and at the same time identify him/her as belonging to a particular group and environment. This growing attention to the stylisation of life forms part of the more general aestheticization of society. Even daily life shows signs of it, with a sharply rising number of people working professionally in fashion, entertainment, art and culture – which have become mass rather than elite sectors. In these contexts a lifestyle acquires the fascination of self-expression, of one's individuality and the desire to emerge from the "grey conformism" of the mass. *Design* confers an aesthetic aura to even the most everyday objects, making them *cult* objects and enriching them with the *function sign* of belonging, of privilege, of allusion and of winking (Baudrillard, 1968). Thus *homo aestheticus* also appears in the world of every day, in the environments of consumption, work, free time, *loisir* and religious behaviour itself. In tandem lifestyles multiply to the extent that one may conclude, as mentioned above, that whereas traditional society had *a* style, modern society has styles of life. In this passage we observe progressive weakening of processes of "vertical" reproduction of the traditional style of life over successive generations.

Every object becomes an ikon-object recounting our relationship with the world, especially with the group to which we belong, acquiring a sacred function. Once again we can see here aesthetics on the wave of "reasons of the heart" and enthusiasm as sources of emotions and passions. It is a cultural climate which, because of its aesthetic dimension, goes beyond generalised rationalisation of existence. The religious field, too, is involved. Practices and liturgical systems are semanticized, becoming a reserve of symbolic meanings, transferring their original meanings to other communications of symbolic meanings and references very different from religious belonging by birth and social standing. Part of liturgical systems has been transformed into a vast system of signification and lifestyles from which everyone can draw a particular, personalised lifestyle.

A lifestyle is derived from the more general aestheticization of society through fashion, consumption, advertising, and seeking after trendy experiences and tendencies. We find again today what Simmel pointed out in his analyses of fashion at the beginning of the twentieth century. The growth of fascination with styles and trends is accompanied by an analogous increase of interest in the aestheticization of reality and in needs, including spiritual needs. Rather than unthinkingly adopting a lifestyle from tradition or habit, the individual constructs her/his own style to express his/her own individuality and planning skill. To trace the history of the invention of *homo aestheticus* and the styles characterizing modernity since the seventeenth century, it is necessary to go from Kant to Hegel to Nietzsche until one arrives at the shifts of post-modernity where new collective rules of life are shaped for democratic individualism and its exaltation of subjects' volition. What effect the fascination of *homo aestheticus* will exercise on the construction of future lifestyles is a new field of research, even for the sciences of religions. Four points may be noted:

1. Aesthetic allure – with unexpected modalities and content – multiplies adherence to cultures outside the great traditions. It is in this phase that the traditional spiritual (and atheism) are changed into forms which are more experiential, individuated and independent from the defined dogmatic contents and borders established by historical religions. It is a direct effect of secularisation understood as the affirmation of the human in all its expressions, *outside* every traditional religious framework and increasingly *beyond* every reference to the divine such as one finds in historical religions. These new spiritual sensibilities take shape in the present religious context, partly denuded of ancient rites and beliefs but at the same time harbingers of a passage to an age characterized by new spiritual symbols and languages.

2. Aesthetics is perceived as a system of sense making an individual's biography plausible to him/herself. This need to "make sense of" individual and collective life is the unexpected datum of the age, which is still undergoing the great social and cultural transformation of modernity. It is through this need for a unitary composition of one's life that new religious alphabets are tried out: new truths, liturgies and practices aimed at endowing daily life with sense. In this spirituality there is something going beyond the observance of rites because it is more concerned with *being* than with *morality*. This new *secular* sensibility is characterized by its sense of acting with the aim of rebuilding what secularisation had fragmented and divided between politics and religion, modernity and tradition, Church and State, workdays

and the Sabbath, and public and private religion; in short, between rationality and transcendence. We are dealing with a multiplicity of situations – involving *ethics, social* environment, *politics, economics* – where the morality of action no longer seems to derive directly from rationality but asks new questions about re-evaluating experience of the *sacred*, about the rebirth of *religiosity*.

3. The tendency of new forms of spirituality is to transform the contents of knowledge, experience and practices from a fixed, substantial form to a mobile one that is continuously expanding. It is the rejection of absolute truths which obstruct development and transformation. Emphasizing experience in every situation means neither more nor less than that. The great dogmas no longer represent eternal thoughts about creation but rather points of passage in an eternal evolution. In modernity's spiritual and social culture the rigid confines of, and links with, the past are loosened. As in continuous seeking, the individual may circulate among the variable multiplicities of life conditions, reflecting upon the *panta rei* of things (Simmel, 2010).

4. The terms "aesthetics" and "experience" recall the Greek *aisthesis*, "perception of the senses", the "sentiment" whose organ, according to Aristotle, was the heart, the word containing a reminder of *aion*, the life principle, the time of existence (Perniola, 2011). *Experience* is the key word both in new spiritualities and in their aesthetic dimension. One wants to "experience" everything. Two concepts in Wilhelm Dilthey's philosophy – *Erlebnis* and *Erfahrung* – are useful in analysing the idea of experience (Dilthey, 1978). In Paolo Jedlowski's explication, *Erlebnis* means individuals' experience in its immediacy and distinctiveness, whereas *Erfahrung* means experience as accumulation and tradition (Jedlowski, 1994). Analysing the two words also helps to analyse the two types of spirituality. *Erfahrung* is the accumulation of experience, which is to say objectified experience. It is what remains of movement, a present past whose events have been consolidated and can be remembered. The noun derives from the verb *erfahren*, meaning to pass through. *Erfahrung* is a tradition which is dilated in time; a process whereby memory is active as the faculty of connecting various lived experiences into a continuity endowed with sense. *Erfahrung* is possible only when accumulated experience exists which helps the individual through life; it is a gift which sediments slowly, and in the past its carriers per excellence were old people. Once this was supported not only by habit but also a symbolic order guaranteed by a ritual system. It is becoming less and less relevant in modernity because the historical conditions which made it possible are lacking. The atrophy of modernity which Walter Benjamin writes about refers to *Erfahrung* understood as long tradition, as memory, as the past synthesized and made available to the present (Benjamin, 2003).

Erlebnis, on the other hand, in a singular sense, is the fulfilment of immediate experience; it has no "collective memory" with which the individual may connect.

The concept of modernity is born at the historical moment when an age identifies with change as a rule, with immediate, lived experience, with "being alive" (*leben*) when something happens, in vividly "being there" (*dasein*). Everything becomes an "experience". Aesthetics is the consumption of immediate experience. There is no "collective memory" for the individual to draw on. The memory of experience does not grow in the humus of a collective memory but is typical of youth generations who find themselves living in situations where the contents of available culture are constantly made meaningless by change. Modernity narrows the spaces of existence, deprives them of their stability and, so, incessantly puts into play unexpected new elements. Sometimes the word *empowerment* is just that, a word, a new ritual whereby individuals cease to be such to acquire a new, transformed identity. We may hypothesize that, in the present phase, these new styles represent a social form of the experience of modernity. But given the importance of the past, how long can the empowerment of these flattened experiences of the present last?

1. *Cities and metropolises*. It was the sociologists of the Chicago School with their interactionistic theories who studied the relations between urban life conditions and the multiplication of lifestyles.[2] Louis Wirth's (1938) well-known essay identified in urbanism a lifestyle of modernity. The city, in the first place, produces objects, behaviour and constructions which turn out to be distinctive more for aesthetic and cultural than for economic functions. For this reason it is natural to expect that in cities modes of behaviour should be formed according to more active and mobile modalities than elsewhere, and that styles of life based on wealth or social class should yield to the more seductive effects of non-stop experimentation stimulated by free time. Special groups and single artists pursue the stylisation of their entire lives in their self-presentation, their look and their differentiation of interests and consumption. Harking back once again to Simmel, if contemporary society portrays itself as the "non-style" society, this is because of the multiplication and exhibition of styles. The stylisation of daily life means that even the most everyday objects, kitsch and behaviour can be incorporated into the world of culture and works of art. It all comes about, however, in a bottomless eclecticism and in that "aesthetic paradigm" which many people today indicate as the distinguishing characteristic of the post-modern. In Italy, too, there are many urban planning practices where religious buildings combine architectural elements associated with traditional theology and new criteria of aestheticizing and semanticizing collective spaces. Indeed the religious dimension embraces different levels: first of all toponymy, in

14   *From a single style to multiple styles*

this case marked by reminders of Catholic traditions; secondly commercial activities close to the Church which reiterate the visibility of Catholic imagery, transforming it into a means of communicating and illustrating a shared identity (Carta, 2011). All of this – as Giuseppe Carta points out – contributes towards creating a territorial identity and answers the need for competition in the religious market. In this attention to urban design and religious franchising can be seen the marketing logic common to churches of all religious traditions.

2. *Reference groups*. A sociological concept which has been connected with lifestyles since their introduction into the discipline is Robert Merton's "groups of reference".[3] They are the groups from which an individual – albeit not *de facto* affiliated – draws inspiration in order to imitate their behaviour, tastes, attitudes and also their "immediate values of reference". Today many lifestyles have their generating element in a reference group encountered online or listening to music. Sometimes these lifestyles anticipate a subsequent real belonging, as happens in forms of "anticipatory socialisation". Research analysing the performative, rather than ascribed, nature of lifestyles in the field of consumption shows to what extent reference groups generate styles (Fabris, 1965). Examination of performative aspects tends to focus on lifestyles' mechanisms of choice, even when conditioned, and therefore the mediation between the socially oriented image proposed by lifestyles and compromise adoption processes conditioned by pre-existent value systems. In general, analysis of reference groups helps to understand how identification with certain groups comes about – groups to which in reality one does not belong – and how styles of life inspired by them are consequently formed. Some individuals act within a social reference framework made up of groups to which they really do belong and others which they imitate. In this way the consumer buys as a function of *both* the belonging group *and* the reference group. Attitudes inspired by the two groups are rarely at odds. These indications are also meaningful in describing lifestyles of a cultural and/or religious kind.

3. *Loisirs*. It was the founder of the sociology of *loisir* (free time), Joffre Dumazedier, who defined lifestyles as the personal way in which each individual organizes daily life, both as environment and as a set of active attitudes (practices) attaining to every group and every subject (Dumazedier, 1967). According to the French sociologist, a lifestyle is not produced mechanically but is rather formed by its modality of initiation, including becoming aware of its characteristics and what it implies in terms of rules and norms. Thus even a style requires effort, self-education and choices. In some cases a lifestyle may even mean a new cognitive-axiological dimension in a context where previously it had been missing. Dumazedier's contribution, through his theoretical and empirical studies, is innovative precisely because

it shows that it is by means of an individual seeking one's own style that *loisirs* acquire their meaning and indicate a system of values. In Dumazedier's last work, *loisirs* are the modalities and contents of *loisir* (Livolsi, 1974). This datum is important both for the analysis of lifestyles in environments where greater availability of free time, increasing possibilities of choice and the more general phenomenon of "the revolution of rising expectations" intensify awareness and the taste of multiple ways of living; and for the interpretation of styles as indicators and containers of their own cognitive-axiological dimension.

4. *Consumption.* A recent perspective of research into the relationship between consumption and lifestyles is to analyse a) consumption as forms of experience and emotion, b) the consumer as an individual chasing dreams, and c) the sites of consumption as places of physical stimulation and aesthetic pleasure. The functions and meanings of consumer practices are transformed, especially in big shopping centres, into gigantic entertainment parks with multiplex cinemas and sports facilities, into scenes of mega-concerts and happenings. Visiting temples of consumption assumes the form of celebrating the cult of *homo consumericus* in the new cathedrals of commerce (Ritzer, 1999). The private sphere, too, has been transformed by the invasion of television advertising and postal catalogues, home shopping and internet. All of which has induced researchers to study the desires and expectations, and the aesthetic and emotional satisfactions, deriving from the experience of consumptions – going beyond the negative considerations typical of mass-consumption theories. In consumption the two dimensions of exploitation and expressiveness have equal weight because, where goods predominate as a sign, consumption, too, is used by individuals as cultural signs with expressive aims. Some important areas of lifestyles – such as evasion, entertainment, shaping and seeking identity, aesthetics, games and recreation – rotate around experience-seeking. At this point one could think ironically that it will be the *homo consumericus* who will mark the supremacy of "being over appearing" – after all the criticism directed towards the society of the *look*.

Notes

1 Berger more than anybody emphasizes the *pluralisation* of the spheres of life and the biographical possibilities characterizing the modern subject (Berger, Berger, and Kellner, 1973).
2 We shall not elaborate here on the Chicago School's research. For them, processes of socialisation – especially those leading to deviancy – are based on principles of symbolic interactionism. The following are worthy of consideration: Lemert, 1967, on the eight degrees of the interaction process leading to secondary deviancy; the passages studied by Becker, 2015; the processes dealt with by Matza,

16 *From a single style to multiple styles*

    1969; and E.H. Sutherland's theory of differentiated association (see also Berzano and Prina, 1995, Chapter 4).
3 The concept of "reference groups", together with "individual reference", was first used by Herbert Hyman (1942); but it was Robert Merton who formed a theory about the relations between behaviour and reference groups (1949).

References

Ansart P. (1999), "Pratique", in P. Ansart, A. Akoun (eds), *Dictionnaire de sociologie*, Le Robert-Seuil, Paris.
Baudrillard J. (1968), *Le système des objets*, Gallimard, Paris (Eng. Trans. *The System of Objects*, Verso, London).
Becker H. S. (2015), *Becoming a Marihuana User*, University of Chicago Press, Chicago.
Benjamin W. (2003), "On the Concept of History", in H. Eiland, M. W. Jennings (eds), *Selected Writings*, Vol. 3, The Belknap Press, Cambridge, MA: 313–355.
Berger P. L., Berger B., Kellner H. (1973), *The Homeless Mind: Modernization and Consciousness*, Penguin Books, Harmondsworth.
Berzano L., Genova C. (2015), *Lifestyles and Subcultures: History and a New Perspective*, Routledge, Abingdon and New York.
Berzano L., Prina F. (1995), *Sociologia della devianza*, Carocci, Roma.
Bourdieu P. (1979), *La distinction. Critique sociale du jugement*, Minuit, Paris (Eng. Trans. *Distincion: A Social Critique of the Judgement of Taste*, Harvard University Press, Cambridge, MA, 1984).
Bourdieu P. (1980), *Le sens pratique*, Minuit, Paris.
Bourdieu P. (1987), *Choses dites*, Minuit, Paris.
Bourdieu P. (2004), *Questions de sociologie*, Minuit, Paris.
Bourdieu P., Passeron J.-C. (1970), *La reproduction. Eléments pour une théorie du système d'enseignement*, Minuit, Paris.
Carta G. (2011), "Rappresentare la società post-secolare: temi e orientamenti della geografia delle religioni", in P. Bonora (ed.), *Rappresentare la territorialità* (Quaderni del territorio, 1), ArchetipoLibri, Bologna.
Dilthey W. (1978), The *Critique of Historical Reason*, University of Chicago Press, Chicago.
Dumazedier J. (1967), *Vers une civilisation du loisir?*, Seuil, Paris (Eng. Trans. *Towards a Society of Leisure*, Free Press, New York).
Elias N. (1987), *Die Gesellschaft der Individuen*, Suhrkamp, Frankfurt (It. Trans. *La società degli individui*, il Mulino, Bologna, 1990: 75–6).
Fabris G. (1965), "Gruppi di riferimento e consumi", *Studi di Sociologia*, III, n. 2: 141–160.
Frisby D. (1985), *Fragments of Modernity*, Polity Press, Oxford.
Giddens A. (1991), *Modernity and Self-Identity: Self and Society in the Late Modern Age*, Polity Press, Cambridge.
Hyman H. H. (1942), *The Psychology of Status*, Columbia University, New York.
Jedlowski P. (1994), *Il sapere dell'esperienza*, Il Saggiatore, Milano.
Jedlowski P. (2003), *Fogli nella valigia*, il Mulino, Bologna.

From a single style to multiple styles 17

Lemert E. M. (1967), *Human Deviance, Social Problems and Social Control*, Prentice-Hall, Englewood Cliffs, NJ (It. Trans. *Devianza, problemi sociali e forme di controllo*, Giuffrè, Milano, 1981).
Livolsi M. (1974), *Sociologie empirique du loisir. Critique et contre-critique de la civilisation du loisir*, Seuil, Paris (It. Trans. *Introduzione a J. Dumazedier, Sociologia del tempo libero*, Franco Angeli, Milano, 1987).
Matza D. (1969), *Becoming Deviant*, Prentice-Hall, Upper Saddle River, NJ (It. Trans. *Come si diventa devianti*, il Mulino, Bologna, 1976).
Merton R. K. (1949), *Social Theory and Social Structure*, The Free Press, Glencoe.
Perniola M. (2011), *Estetica contemporanea*, il Mulino, Bologna.
Ritzer G. (1999), *Enchanting a Disenchanted World*, Sage, Thousand Oaks, CA.
Simmel G. (1890), *Über die soziale Differenzierung. Soziologische und psychologische Untersuchungen*, Duncker & Humblot, Leipzig.
Simmel G. (1896–97), "Comment les formes sociales se maintiennent", *L'Année Sociologique*, I: 71–109.
Simmel G. (1900), *Philosophie des Geldes*, Duncker & Humblot, Leipzig (Eng. Trans. *Philosophy of Money*, Routledge, New York, 1978).
Simmel G. (1908), "Das Problem des Stiles", *Dekorative Kunst. Illustrierte Zeitschrift für angewandte Kunst*, XVI, n. 7: 307–316.
Simmel G. (2010), *Denaro e vita. Senso e forme dell'esistere*, F. Mora (ed.), Mimesis, Milano.
Weber M. (1922), *Wirtschaft und Gesellschaft*, Tübingen, Mohr (Eng. Trans. *Economy and Society*, University of California Press, Berkeley, 1978).
Weber M. (2011), *Methodology of Social Sciences*, Transaction Publishers, New Brunswick.
Wirth L. (1938), "Urbanism as a Way of Life", *American Journal of Sociology*, XLIV, n. 1: 1–24.

2 Spiritual revolution
Multiplication of forms

What has been said hitherto can also be applied to the religious field when we consider that a style, rather than referring only to daily practices and consumption, above all concerns the identities of individuals and *who* they are in the *secular* society. In the 1960s, a period of massive mobilisation and conflicts began in the West: student protests, workers' struggles, movements in favour of rights, migratory flows and recognition of new gender identities. In the spiritual world too, a long "state of gestation" was initiated. It was Max Weber (1922) who, by means of this concept, indicated the ferments which can be observed in periods of maximum creativity. Great innovations and transformations are generated by the power of groups of phenomena "in a state of gestation" which are translated into forms of cultural, social, economic and spiritual invention. It is in the "state of gestation" that the generative capacity of an individual or collective charism starts a new world. We may consider 1968 as the beginning of a spiritual revolution and the start of the *secular* age.

The unexpected datum from this age is the multiplication of spiritualities, proof that the future is not always and/or necessarily an extension of already-existent tendencies. Marcel Mauss had made this point, observing that variations in collective mentality somewhat resemble the movement of a pendulum which, after a decisive movement in one direction, does the same in the opposite direction (Mauss, 1923–24). Primitive thought is not simply that which preceded modern scientific thought; sometimes they are parallel thoughts. This explains the foretold disappearance of religions in past decades and the unexpected vitality of religion today. But one never returns to the same point, even with regard to religious phenomena; which demonstrates the present metamorphosis of the religious in its forms, beliefs and symbols. When historical religions are no longer capable of satisfying the needs and expectations of individuals, they form others. When the pendulum oscillates too much in the direction of fanatic theism and of superstition, an opposite movement of rejection of every kind of transcendence takes place. And, finally, when there is a perceived hint that nothing is sacred any more, or worthy of respect, and everything is a sign of Something Else, then new gods and rituals take shape. And this is the situation where the feeling that something "absent" pursues us is most intense.

> When the gods abandon the world and religions cease to signify their otherness, it is the world itself which begins to appear "other" and to show an imaginative depth, which becomes the object of specific research endowed with an end in itself and referring only to itself. The simple fact is that imaginative perception of the reality which made up the anthropological content of religious activity starts functioning on its own, independently of the ancient contents which channelled it.
> (Gauchet, 1992: 297 [our translation])

When the gods evoked by Marcel Gauchet abandon the world, where do spiritual forms – and those of atheism – go? It is an important question because it was formulated by the most radical scholar of the "religious after religions" theory (Gauchet, 1992; Ferry and Gauchet, 2004). To express it simply, we may answer that they transfer to *secular* forms since the current age which determines them is *secular*. It is in this *secular* phase, when the individual considers that s/he has total power over him/herself, that the traditional spiritual and atheism change, as has been said, into personal experiential forms independent of historical religions' defined dogmatic contents and borders. It is the anthropological condition which Max Weber would call "a feeling of unprecedented inner loneliness of the single individual" (1904–05: 104) connected with the great historical-religious process of disenchantment of the world which began with ancient Hebrew prophesies and, united to Greek philosophical thought and later to modernity, rejected as superstition all magical means of seeking salvation.

Historically this polymorphic redefinition of the divine and the spiritual in relation to personal and collective life came about around the end of the last century, a period which scholars have already defined as *spiritual revolution* (Heelas and Woodhead, 2005). Therefore it is difficult to understand theories based on the principle of the inexorable decline of religion. Even the dissemination factors of new spiritualities do not lead to the disappearance of the religious experience; they rather indicate its continual redefinition. Researchers are left with the task of understanding individuals' spiritual dimension – which today, however, seems to be *outside* every traditional religious framework and increasingly *beyond* every reference to the divine as found in historical religions.

This section will present three transformations at the origin of this present phase: spiritual individuation, the revolution of rising spiritual expectations and multiple identities.

Spiritual individualisation

In analysis of religious phenomena there is growing attention to the concepts of privatisation and individualisation: frequent use is made of expressions such as private religion, designer spirituality, DIY religion, *à la carte* and so on. What has been scarcely examined, however, is the concept of distinction and individuation. Talking about distinction means referring to a process by means of which an individual, or a collectivity, affirms a difference, and therefore establishes a border, between himself/herself/themselves and others. The fact that a spirituality's significant practices reveal elements with different purposes means that those who adopt them consider them unifying traits which they share but at the same time separate them from those who are not in agreement. From this point of view, we proceed on the basis of a definition of distinction as complementary to and directly connected with that of imitation: separation and linkage, differentiation and cohesion. Through some significant practices the individual, on one hand, signals her/his affinity to other individuals more-or-less clearly perceived as belonging to a common spirituality while, on the other, also signalling distance from other groups. But signalling affinity is never total because the individual in any case retains a distinction need.

In this sense it is possible to consider three different relationships among *I*, *we* and *others*: 1) *I* establishes a relationship of identification with a *we*; 2) *We*, and *I* as part of the *we*, establishes a relationship of distinction from the *others*; 3) *I* establishes a relationship of individuation with regard to *we*, thereby tending to preserve one's own individuality.

This notion of distinction thus interpreted recalls Carl Gustav Jung's concept of individuation, which we can adopt here as the characterizing element of new spiritualities. The multiplication of spiritualities outside the great religious traditions, which widens the gap between organized religions and individual spiritualities, is partly a consequence of the growth of spiritual individuation needs.

In the 1920s Jung introduced the concept of individuation whereby the individual brings the *I* and the Self closer together. In this kind of "spiritual voyage" towards a greater consciousness of Self, one passes through the various stages of the Shadow, the *Anima* and the *Animus*, and then the Wise Old Wo/Man, finally to reach the Self as the arrival point of individuation, unfolding before the individual like a blossoming flower (Jung, 1921). The archetype of the Self which symbolizes the same individual is depicted as light, as mandala, as a set of four, as a circle, and as God. According to Jung, individuation is how much each one of us is called upon to do in order to develop one's individual personality, differentiating oneself from the others. Although it is an "individual way", which may lead one to travel along

Spiritual revolution 21

paths very different from the customary ones, it cannot but recognize collective norms. There is no individuation path which has as its final destination estrangement from (or destruction of) the social fabric.

Jung's individuation is of interest in this book because it constitutes a form of spiritual differentiation resulting in the development of a style of life which is representative of a particular spirituality. Although it is an "individual way" characterized by innovative – sometimes deviant – elements, individuation may both still share more general norms and values (as is the case of spiritualities within historical religions) and yet still consider itself as being totally autonomous and independent. In both cases individuation represents a form of spiritual elevation leading to an extension of the sphere of consciousness. "Individuation coincides with the evolution of consciousness from its original *identity state*; thus individuation represents an expansion of the sphere of consciousness and of conscious psychological life" (ibid.: 465 [our translation]). Jung also talks about it in The Red Book (Liber Novus) written between 1913 and 1930, which he considered an exercise in "active imagination" and a tool for discovery and extension of the unconscious: "No one has my God, but my God has everyone, including me" (Jung, The Red Book, 2010: 245 [our translation]).

What effects has Jung's individuation had in the present phase? Three may be indicated: the first is relative to the current *secular* context in which it takes place; the second concerns its expansion also in the spiritual field; and the third is the nature of its development, similar to that of the passage from a *style* to *styles* of life.

1. The present historical context fuelling individuation is one of immediate experiences, a concept which we have already seen. In traditional society, on the other hand, spiritualities took the form of "long spiritual traditions" composed of values, knowledge, behavioural norms, languages and symbols. One belonged to them either as a result of a long socialisation process or of conversion. Today, on the contrary, there is a prevalence of spiritualities consisting of more immediate and interactionistic elements, as happens with "short traditions". They are spiritualities seeking more direct, spontaneous and profound spiritual experience (Roof, 1999: 86). In the spiritual field, too, these new spiritualities radicalise the individual's right to choose. A particular historical turning point between the two forms occurred in Christian churches in the decades following the 1960s (Vatican Council II 1962–65, Protests of 1968). It was in that period that change became the rule and the image of continuity was seen to collapse – the continuity which was the symbolic spiritual armour of traditional spiritualities. In the name of individual autonomy and the rights of subjectivity, the authorities who expected to impose norms of conscience and behaviour were called into question.

22 *Spiritual revolution*

It should be recognized, however, that still today some of these new spiritualities are being enriched by normative and universal elements, being transformed into something that makes sense not only to one person but to everybody, according to a form of development which scholars call *objectivisation*, which is the way in which the meanings of actions come to have common sense, the same for everybody (Berger and Luckmann, 1966, Chapter I). Spiritualities, too, may be objectivised, with practices and symbols shared not only by those who have produced them but by a common world. Religions, in particular, are nothing if not sets of objectivisations in believing, in praying, in behaving in a community. The main example of objectivisation is the production of (linguistic, corporeal and ritual) signs in religious ceremonies, in celebrating common feast-days, in expressing one's beliefs. Even new spiritualities may become shared thanks to linguistic, corporeal and ritual meanings shared with others. In this objectivisation of things which goes beyond the here and now, there is a certain form of transcendence exceeding daily life which, especially in relation to the spiritual and religious environment, evokes other spatial, temporal and social dimensions.

2. The second datum is the constant increase of forms of individuation even in the religious field. Through these, an ever-greater number of individuals tries out other alphabets of the religious: truths, rituals, liturgies and practices designed to inform daily life with sense. Whether traditional or new, the spiritual practices make individuals' biographies plausible and meaningful. To sum up their innovative nature we may refer to the tendency to transfer the contents of knowledge, experiences and practices from a fixed, substantial form to a new, mobile form which is continuously expanding and renouncing absolute truths which would impede further evolutions. Recalling Simmel (2010) once again, one may say that in today's spirituality there is an "objectivity of the style" and that this objectivity transforms spiritualities into lifestyles. The objectivity and impersonal nature of spiritualities allow their adaptation to a greater number of people. This is the very course of fashion. Even Simmel considered styles and fashions as "functional equivalents" because both perform socialisation and individuation functions.

3. A spiritual individuation produces forms with few rules and a lot of choice, in a trend similar to what happens in the passage from *a style* to *styles* of life. Spiritual practices acquire the characteristics of objectivity, placing themselves "at the disposal" of whoever adopts them; everyone makes one's own use of them, connoting them with personal meanings and functions independently of their original cognitive-axiological dimension. Those who adopt such practices cannot understand the idea of a spirituality which does not fully reflect their own lives and sensibilities. In the past, spiritualities

welled up in reaction to the mainstream of all the great religions, and they worked well for lives with different sensibilities without breaking away from their churches of reference. But today this differentiation is particularly radical; linking up with contemporary individualism, it does not cancel religion or make it irrelevant but rather reproduces it everywhere in a potentially unlimited form of pluralism (Taylor, 2007, Part IV).

In traditional society it was religious institutions which produced individual identities; today it is often individual identities in reciprocal interaction which produce religious institutions such as the new spiritualities. Here the question arises of recognition and validation of these spiritualities. Religion, too, is a system where each particular element (groups, the faithful, practices, beliefs, experiences and so on) receives its distinctive value from its relationship with the other elements, especially with those which have the power to legitimate it. The relationship between historical religions and new spiritualities is precisely that between behaviour legitimated by religious institutions and individually legitimated behaviour – or legitimated by consonance with other behaviour. Here we refer particularly to the US sociologists W.C. Roof and R. Wuthnow. In this connection, see also Danièle Hervieu-Léger (1999, Chapter IV).

Revolution of rising spiritual expectations

In the last decades of the twentieth century a "silent revolution" took place, witnessing a sudden increase in economic and cultural opportunities and an analogous increase of new needs and expectations on the part of movements, groups and individuals. In those years there was a multiplication of mobilisation on behalf of social services, minority rights claims, demands for equal opportunities for women and, in general, the formation of new social movements rotating around the most variegated themes.

The scientific reference is to Ronald Inglehart's (1977) research and his typology of three areas of needs: the area of *having* (needs which orient the choice of materialistic lifestyles); the area of *being* (self-fulfilment and citizenship needs); and the area of *loving* (relational and quality-of-life needs). Each of these three areas changes considerably in relation to the structural and socio-cultural characteristics of each individual and group of belonging. In the period mentioned the explosion of needs was precisely that of the third area, upon which "the return of the subject" was based. So the individual came back after an age when social and economic structures, parties, trade unions and institutions occupied centre stage.

That revolution, which began with the student protests in 1968, also affected the religious field. The set of needs, aspirations and spiritual practices (made less dependent upon official religions by the general secularisation of society) appeared in a form which we may define as the "revolution of rising expectations" (Berzano, 2014). Even among the faithful of the various churches new interests emerged, new needs and demands, giving rise to a different spiritual sensibility. In the religious field, too, there re-appeared a multiple subject who identified with his/her religion in various ways according to the changes to which s/he was subjected – a plural *spiritual I* which no longer referred to only one permanent essence but to a process of successive spiritual identifications.

The disintegration of the metaphysical concept of a religious subject led to a rethinking of spiritual identity too as a field of possibilities and choices. Everything recalled the 1930s social-psychology figure of the marginal man and the marginal man theory which indicated the differentiated identity of the modern individual, belonging at the same time – whether by choice or not – to more than one circle or various social worlds: working, residential, cultural, sporting and also religious (Park, 1928). Today the "return of the subject" has had its effect also in the religious field, with a pluralisation of the forms of lifestyles on the level of public social conduct, on the level of consciousness and in the dichotomy between public and private spheres (Berger, Berger, and Kellner, 1973). This habit of the subject to make "successive choices" was facilitated by the secular condition of life where religion was more relevant to aims of personal perfection than to those of social order.

The result is *differentiated subjectivity* even in the religious field, almost as if to avoid the unique content of an individual life's fragmenting into the objectified forms of institutional theology. In the dynamics of religious forms too, one may glimpse the unquiet presence of the subject who sees her/his autonomy threatened and intends to free him/herself from the obligation to follow unthinkingly ways of life transmitted by tradition or habit. In this process of stylistic personalisation religious individuals grow without a fixed *status* but rather seeking self-fulfilment through creativity and new experiences. Thus none of this heralds the end of religious lifestyles but rather the multiplication of their forms. We can observe a conception of religious life which tends to adopt its own coordinates of content, form and interest for different spiritual traditions.

Research into the religious belonging of citizens of Christian-majority countries reveals that a nett distinction between "Christians" and "non-religious" is inaccurate (Houtman and Mascini, 2002). Other types of belonging can rather be identified: those who have a high level of affinity with spirituality, but not with Christian churches; those who have a high level of affinity with Christian churches, but not with spirituality; and those who have a low level of affinity with both. From this point of view the secularisation process and its final result – *secularity* – work in such a way that nothing which has been secularised disappears but takes the form of a new element which has separated from another element. Thus the sacred separates from the profane, the civil from the ecclesial, the practical from the functional, the innovative from the traditional, and so on with further differentiations. It follows that this age's "spiritual provisions", and social and cultural conditions, are no longer those of the age when secularisation began.

All of this brings about a situation (even among historical religions) of differentiation where many see the volatilisation of faiths without belief and without religion, the multiplication of apparently atheistic practices. For this very reason everybody revives new identity, autonomy and unity needs; and at the same time proposes new forms of re-composition of one's religious system and of mutation of the self, with a transition towards other religious systems (Quack, Schuh, 2017).

For historical religions this *secular* condition is characterized by all the secularisation effects mentioned as well as by all the new spiritual supply which living in the age of secularity makes available. New spiritualities, too, are a result connected with the effects of religious *secularity*, which has stimulated socialisation processes alternative to those whose centrality in recent centuries has determined secularisation. These new spiritualities cannot always be traced back to univocally determined subjectivities; in other words, secularisation does not always produce similar subjects. This, too, is an effect of the loss of centrality which secularisation, understood as differentiation, has caused.

Multiple spiritual identities

In the religious field too, contemporary identities become multiple, varying over time and identifying with one's religion in different ways according to the everyday worlds where one happens to live. They are plural spiritual identities which no longer refer to only one permanent essence but to a series of successive identifications. As we have seen, the dissolution of a metaphysical idea of the religious subject leads to the consideration of spiritual identity as a field of possibilities and limits contemporaneously belonging to different social worlds: working, residential, cultural, sporting and also religious. This multiple identity is significantly related to religious lifestyles which, insofar as they are real experience of the self in various social situations, are in their turn open, differentiated and reflexive. Such a phenomenology of *successive choices* is particularly favoured by the present context in which, as we have seen, religion is relevant more to objectives of personal completion than to those of social order.

In this scenario it is not difficult to sense the same functions and dynamics as are active in the formation of lifestyles, which are developing increasingly with the progressive reduction of control imposed on the individual by fundamental social institutions. It is the new aspiration towards self-expression, partly the fruit of the gains made by social movements – not only workers but also pacifists, feminists and ecologists – and of new religions.

One of the decisive turning points between *style* and *styles* was in the decades following 1968. In that period of accelerated modernisation there was a proliferation of new forms of belonging, of belief, of practice, of values, and of spiritual interests and tastes, traceable to a growing pluralisation of religious models. The molecular nature of these transformations affected equally the life of the individual and the life of institutions. Focussed research has documented this transformation, introducing terms such as "implicit religion", "scenery religion", "multiple forms of pluralism", "designer religion" and "secular spiritualities". From the above we observe the emergence of religious lifestyles independent not only from socio-economic status but also from the individual's primary/institutional religious belonging. In this reading, lifestyles are a source of identity and autonomy. Besides, the very identity of today's individuals no longer depends only on past history but is more and more built actively on a foundation of autonomous cultural and symbolic resources.

It is in this social and cultural environment that religious forms recently termed "designer religion" by scholars become defined: a religion where personal taste, intellectual content and aesthetic forms integrate to compose a personal ideal of religion (Berzano, 2014). Whoever seeks such a religious profile also intends to choose its contents on the basis of one's personal sensibility. This is a key to interpret individuals' growing tendency to pursue their own spiritual preferences. It is not only a question of those who wish to construct their personal faith in God but also of those who claim adherence to a traditional religion while loosening links with its traditional beliefs and rites. In this sense designer religion is unceasingly creative, trendy, eclectic and reflexive. Those who live it consider it possible both to belong to a historical religion and to attribute personal meaning to its transmitted beliefs and rituals. In designer religion, understood as the construction of one's own religious lifestyle, we find once again repeated what happened in the construction of lifestyles through consumption, artistic preferences and the use of free time.

Conclusion

The power of the spiritual transformations of which we have spoken – reminding us of more general transformations between belief and non-belief, the sacred and the profane – is such that various scholars have been induced to re-introduce the "pivotal age" concept for our historical phase.

The reference is to the period which Karl Jaspers, in his 1949 text *Vom Ursprung und Ziel der Geschichte*, defined as an "axial age". The German philosopher was indicating the last millennium before Christ, during which there appeared in different civilisations various "superior" forms of worldview and religious experiences, at first independent one from the other but in reality setting up a kind of "axis" thanks to thinkers such as Confucius, the Buddha, Socrates and the Hebrew prophets. Today post-axial religions – especially Christianity, with its hegemony in the West and the secularising effects of its message – indicate as salvation the (almost categorical) imperative of constructing the world and one's own life by means of self-fulfilment, self-improvement. It is the human aspiration to imitate the absolute goodness of the divine in opposing and containing the inevitability of chaos, injustice and death.

The three carriers of enlightened critical spirit, individualisation and globalisation are the sources of this great current transformation of cultural and religious awareness. All three have facilitated the passage from a society where it was all but impossible *not* to believe in God to one in which religious faith is no longer taken for granted even among believers themselves – but is conceived of as *one* among the possible choices. The result is a different framework of religious interests in their connections with the world: a re-evaluation of experiences of the divine, the rebirth of multiple religiosities, and new ethicality demands and needs. For this reason the mass religious freedom of individuals with respect to their original religions of affiliation ever-increasingly assumes the form of a new ethical and cultural sensibility, including the new premise of lay culture according to which all religious options are – both *de facto* and *de jure* – reciprocally equivalent.

As we have already seen, the weakening of "vertical" reproduction processes of cultural models (and their relative institutions) through the generations is particular to this condition of life. A society results which lacks by-birth, collectively shared imagery: almost an "anomic society" like that which concerned founders of social sciences such as Émile Durkheim over a century ago. Also values, attitudes and (including religious) lifestyles are today less connected with traditional affiliations – one of which being social classes themselves – and more and more with individual biographical choices. The result is an extension of the possibilities of choice left to the individual as well as a weakening of points of reference on the basis of which such choices may be matured. This means a "horizontal society" where identities and belongings are less and less ascribed – which is to say, inherited by birth – and increasingly depend on individuals' spontaneous initiative, but become, as a consequence, weaker, more problematic and reflexive. The passage is from a society with *a style* to a society with *styles* (Berzano and Genova, 2011, 2015).

Based on this environment, greater interest grows in questions concerning the sense of life, the rediscovery of the Self, encounters with the others, elsewhere and the beyond. These themes engage the individual in his/her relationship with existence and provoke questions about sense which flow from that relationship with existence – especially in the context of post-secular society characterized by the redefinition of the religious too. They are the spiritualities whose practices are generated in individuals' daily lives, independently of the religion of belonging and in forms of personal or collective ethics which give a sense to life.

These last spiritualities can also be found among those belonging to religions. All the spiritualities have in common that their barycentre can no longer be collocated in an instituted religion from which it receives recognition and validation. The individual adopts them, questions, evaluates and personalises them according to her/his sensibilities. In the multiplication of these spiritual sensibilities there seems to exist, on the part of individuals, widespread "low-intensity" interest in many diverse areas; which later becomes "high-intensity" in one area in particular which they find richer in emotions and in answers. This, too, is a trait of the general "convergence culture" (the culture of the future, some say): convergence between knowledge, markets, technologies, media – and also among religions (Jenkins, 2006). This form of religious pluralism, the right to believe in everything or nothing, is making itself felt today in Europe as it has always done in the United States. From the American model Europe is also adopting "community individuality" where, for example, one loves vast religious gatherings but in one's daily life one marches to the beat of one's interior drummer. The tendency is to adapt even spirituality to one's sensibility as one does with clothes, homes, consumption and social activities. It is a great inversion with respect to the decline of the moral absolutism of religions which preach first of all The Ten Commandments, a sense of guilt, sin, judgement. This disappearance of moral absolutism and faith in a transcendent God is the basis of the need for a new paradigm, one which will fill the vacuum of life and constitute a new source of sense.

References

Berger P. L., Berger B., Kellner H. (1973), *The Homeless Mind: Modernization and Consciousness*, Penguin Books, Harmondsworth.
Berger P. L., Luckmann T. (1966), *The Social Construction of Reality*, Doubleday and Co., New York (It. Trans. *La realtà come costruzione sociale*, il Mulino, Bologna, 1969).
Berzano L. (2014), *Spiritualità senza Dio?*, Mimesis, Milano.
Berzano L., Genova C. (2011), *Sociologia dei lifestyles*, Carocci, Roma.

Spiritual revolution 29

Berzano L., Genova C. (2015), *Lifestyles and Subcultures: History and a New Perspective*, Routledge, Abingdon and New York.
Ferry L., Gauchet M. (2004), *Le Religieux après la religion*, Grasset, Paris.
Gauchet M. (1992), *Il disincanto del mondo: una storia politica della religione*, Einaudi, Torino.
Heelas P., Woodhead L. (2005), *The Spiritual Revolution: Why Religion Is Giving Way to Spirituality*, Wiley-Blackwell, Oxford and Malden.
Hervieu-Léger D. (1999), *Le pèlerin et le converti: la religion en mouvement*, Flammarion, Paris.
Houtman D., Mascini P. (2002), "Why Do Churches Become Empty, While New Age Grows? Secularization and Religious Change in the Netherlands", *Journal for the Scientific Study of Religion*, XLI, n. 3: 455–473.
Inglehart R. (1977), *The Silent Revolution*, Princeton University Press, Princeton (It. Trans. *La rivoluzione silenziosa*, ed. M. Rodriguez, Rizzoli, Milano, 1983).
Jaspers K. (1949), *Vom Ursprung und Ziel der Geschichte*, Piper, München (Eng. Trans. *The Origin and Goal of History*, Routledge, Oxon, 1953).
Jenkins H. (2006), *Convergence Culture: Where Old and New Media Collide*, New York University Press, New York and London.
Jung C. G. (1921), *Psychologische Typen*, Rascher, Zürich (Eng. Trans. *Psychological Types*, Princeton University Press, Princeton, 1990).
Jung C. G. (2010), *Il libro rosso: liber novus*, Bollati Boringhieri, Torino (Original Edition *Das rote Buch: liber novus*, Patmos Verlag, Düsseldorf, 2009; Eng. Trans. *Red Book for Our Time*, Chiron, Asheville, 2009).
Mauss M. (1923–24), "Essai sur le don. Forme et raison de l'échange dans les sociétés archaïques", *L'Année Sociologique*, 2me série (included in *The Gift: The Form and Reason for Exchange in Archaic Societies*, Routledge, New York, 1954).
Park R. (1928), "Human Migration and the Marginal Man", *American Journal of Sociology*, XXXIII, n. 6: 881–893.
Quack J., Schuh C. (eds) (2017), *Religious Indifference: New Perspectives From Studies on Secularization and Nonreligion*, Springer, Dodrecht.
Roof W. C. (1999), *Spiritual Marketplace: Baby Boomers and the Remaking of American Religion*, Princeton University Press, Princeton.
Simmel G. (2010), *Denaro e vita. Senso e forme dell'esistere*, Mimesis, Milano.
Taylor C. (2007), *A Secular Age*, Harvard University Press, Cambridge, MA.
Weber M. (1922), *Wirtschaft und Gesellschaft*, Mohr, Tübingen.

3 The fourth secularisation

The great transformation of Western societies which social sciences have defined as secularisation and disenchantment recalls Max Weber's classic works on the rise of capitalism and modernity. A great deal of research has analysed its consequent effect on economics, on culture, on the political organization of societies and on religion. Every secularisation represents a new autonomy of reality, which previously depended strictly on the religious; thus a passage from *sacrum* to *saeculum*, from the sacred to the secular.

The aim of this chapter is to integrate the fundamental works of social sciences about secularisation with the further contribution which can be found particularly in the French school of ancient Greek history starting from Jean-Pierre Vernant, Marcel Detienne, Françoise Frontisi-Ducroux, Pierre Vidal-Naquet and other scholars of Greek myths and thought (Vernant, 1965, 1985, 1989, 1990; Detienne and Vernant, 1974, 1979; Frontisi-Ducroux and Vernant, 1997; Vernant and Vidal-Naquet, 1972, 1986). On the basis of their research a first secularisation was identified (which will be dealt with in the following sub-section *From mythos to Logos*) as the passage from the universe of Greek mythology to that of the philosophy of the *Logos*. A second, later secularisation was the passage from *Logos* to Christianity (see eponymous sub-section). The secularisation studied by Weber, the advent of modernity which gradually makes contexts of thought autonomous of religion increasingly numerous, is the third (see sub-section *Modernity and scientific autonomy*).

But what has happened from the mid-twentieth century onwards, after the secularisation analysed by Weber had helped to make religions less and less relevant in the public sphere? The hypothesis here (proposed in the sub-section *Autonomy of lifestyles*) is that the form of a fourth – more radical – secularisation may be introduced: that of daily life and of lifestyles. The autonomy of lifestyles, asserted by Max Weber's secularisation, has spread to the autonomy of individual practices "from the cradle to the grave". In this context the world of needs, individual expectations and everyday practices is becoming more and more a world of freedom and autonomy from religion.

This third section will begin by presenting classical Greek philosophy as the secularisation of the preceding mythology by a rational reformulation of the great myths hinging on Aristotle's *abstract Logos* concept shared by the Stoics. Acting in an analogous way, Christianity substituted the *abstract Logos* with the *Logos-Man*. On the theoretical level, therefore, there was a double revolution: on one hand the divine (the *Theion*), from being an anonymous supreme principle, becomes a person; on the other, the way to know this person is no longer reason but faith. The *Theion*, which in Greek philosophy was understood as *Logos* and *Cosmos*, in Christianity became the *divine-humanity*. The imposition of the Christian vision was the second secularisation, which we may term "humanisation of the divine" (Ferry, 1996, 2008).

Sociologists have mainly paid attention to a third secularisation which took place from the fourteenth century onwards, first with Humanism, then with Cartesian and Hegelian Rationalism and up to twentieth-century philosophy: the secularisation of sciences – economic, political and natural, and later psychological, anthropological and sociological. Modernity, capitalism, individual rights and religious freedom sprang from this secularisation. The "City of Man" asserted its autonomy. This turning – which Max Weber called *disenchanting/disenchantment* of the world – came about in the West as a result of the meeting between great socio-economic transformations and the Protestant ethic. The disenchanted man (coinciding in Weber with the man who has a vocation for a sober, virtuous ethic) built the secular world. In the same period the Dutch philosopher Hugo Grotius formulated the principle of the autonomy of natural right, valid in itself whether or not God exists (*etsi deus non daretur*).

The section will conclude with the hypothesis of a fourth secularisation concerning the contemporary age. It is the secularisation of lifestyles which decreasingly depend upon individuals' religion of belonging and increasingly upon their autonomous choices. The result is a "horizontal religion" within which individuals' identities and belongings derive more and more from their personal initiatives, becoming, however, increasingly reflexive and problematic.

From *mythos* to *Logos*

Greek philosophy arose out of the rational reformulation of the great Greek myths. The history of the West, too, began with Greek thought which, in a "lay" manner, recovered and secularised the earlier myths, then developed into the great philosophical tradition of wisdom and harmony of the world with Parmenides, Plato, Aristotle and the Stoics (Vernant, 1989, 1990; Detienne and Vernant, 1974). It all began about eleven centuries before Christ in an environment where myths, religious interpretations of the world and the genealogy of the Gods were the "mythological dome" under which mortals lived their lives. Writing in the Iliad about this period and the Trojan War, Homer narrates the constant presence of the Gods in the affairs of men – a passionate, loving, furious presence, sometimes envious of men's happiness.

In the cities absolute power was exercised by the king (*anax*), political leader and highest priest, who – assisted by a priestly caste – established the calendar of rites. His was an exclusive, charismatic power; he alone was in touch with the Gods through mysterious, secret rites (Vernant, 1962). Around the tenth century A.D. Dorian migrations began to provoke the first transformations. The city, with its new social forces, started to replace the king as the centre of power. Religion, too, felt the effects of these changes, and the Gods, who had been presences influencing real life, began to appear more like symbols, images, representations of the sacred. Little by little history and thought became more autonomous from the Gods and from their mythologies. It was the initiation of the first secularisation: from the mythological period of the *sacrum* to the secular period of the *saeculum*. Greek philosophy was born from this in the framework of specific forms of collective life, religious attitude and thought.

In the fifth century B.C. Protagoras, father of the Sophists, wrote: "With regard to the Gods, I am not certain whether they exist or do not exist, or what they look like; indeed there are many things which impede certain knowledge in this respect, mainly the obscurity of the object and the brevity of human life" (Untersteiner, 1967, Vol. 1: 79, 4). Protagoras's surprising "agnosticism" indicates that an entire process – which we here call secularisation – had reached its conclusion.[1] Further proof can be found in Hesiod's poems *Theogony* and *Works and Days* (written between the eighth and seventh centuries B.C.), where the Gods are still present but their action is ever-more distant, abstract and mediated by law, by the idea of justice and by the institutions of men. By now the Gods pass judgement through tribunals.

As an example of the secularisation process (already under way in Hesiod's time), we may consider two significant elements to be found in the *Eumenides* (458 B.C.), the third play (the other two being *Agamemnon* and *Libation Bearers*) of the Aeschylus tragic trilogy known collectively as the *Oresteia* (D'Agostini, 2016). The first element is the acceptance of, and respect for, the Areopagus (court) sentence passed by the Furies/Eumenides and all the citizens; the second is the effective use of *Logos* – reason, persuasion, the arts of rhetoric – by Athena to convince the Furies. *Logos* as reason sets ancient Greece out on the road to secularisation. Soon afterwards came the affair of Antigone and the law of nature which the heroine asserts will be a kind of natural law ahead of its time.

> In Protagoras reflection on the divine is transformed into an object of investigation like any other, distinguished only by its being "obscure", "obscure" here implying the impossibility of empirical-scientific investigation, the impossibility of "seeing", "hearing" or touching the God, who is a wan descendent of the Gods who were "seen", "heard" and "touched" by men in Homer. The separation of the human from the divine is sanctioned by the scarce semantic possibilities of the term "God". The God who came down from Olympus or the Goddess who seized Achilles's hair, the participant God whether friendly or unfriendly, flowed back into a completely different verbal class. The God of antiquity is dead. Fifth-sixth century Greece celebrated the first "death of God" in Western history.
>
> (ibid.: 4)

Protagoras's investigatory logic presupposes a separation between the person who investigates – who posits him/herself as the subject in the knowledge process – and God as the object of the wo/man's investigation. Religion has become an object of investigation, a set of beliefs, rituals and dogmas which can be analysed in their social function.[2] Life, at first intimately religious, becomes secular. Since the terms of contraposition between society (as intellectual, logical-formal mediation of reality) and nature (as immediate representation of reality) is repeated between religion and philosophical thought, religion is combined with the social function and linked, as by a double thread, with political power.[3] Thus the birth of Greek philosophy was accompanied by the philosophical "death" of a model of religion and the ancient Gods – not the end of religion but its radical transformation and the advent of a never-before-seen model of the sacred and of humanity. The *Logos* appeared to fill the vacuum left by the Gods. With the Sophists in the fifth century B.C. Greek philosophy became the antinormative summit of the religious, morality and ethics, and was to oblige each individual to accept responsibility for her/his own life.

Following Jean-Pierre Vernant's (1990) thought, one can say that Greek mythology is summed up in two fundamental works: Hesiod's *Theogony* and Homer's *Odyssey*. In them one can find the two central constitutive messages which Greek philosophy renewed from the fifth century, secularising them, and which Christianity later radically secularised. Indeed, it was to be Christianity which would – some centuries later – master Greek secularisation.

The first message of the secularised mythology – the nascent philosophy – is that the world is no longer *Chaos* but *Cosmos*: an organized world with its just, good, harmonious order. The gods of *Chaos* and war – Titans and Cyclopes, enemies of order and harmony – fade. This secularisation of mythology by philosophy comes about through some recurrent ideas. Leaving *Chaos* behind enables humanity to live its existence according to a predestined cosmic order, overcoming the fear of death. Re-establishing harmony between one's self and one's world of life, of birth (for Ulysses the longing to return home), is each person's dearest wish. And the idea that the cosmos is eternal means that humans may consider themselves fragments of eternity as long as they adapt to its laws.

The second message of Greek philosophy is that a good life overcomes the fear of death – not only one's own but that of one's nearest and dearest. A wise person conquers fear because s/he knows that it is due to fear that one loses one's freedom of thought and one's openness towards other people. Furthermore, profound anguish linked to the past or the future prevents one from living in the present, the only dimension in which it is possible to live (the Roman poet Horace's *Carpe diem*).

The two messages of secularised mythology were to be developed later, especially in Stoicism, into an equivalence among *Cosmos*, *Logos* (the well-organized, logical, rational world) and *Theion* (the divine). *Theion* is perfect cosmic order because it is just and transcendent with respect to humanity. We did not create this perfect cosmic order: it is eternal, superior to us and divine (*theion*). The *Cosmos* is at the same time *Logos* (rational) and *Theion* (divine). What, then, is a well-lived life in this vision of Greek philosophy? It is one which accepts its own finitude, death as a natural condition, but aspires to live in harmony with the cosmos and find one's place in the order of the cosmos. Life in harmony with cosmic order allows overcoming the fear of death and living in the present with the attitude which Nietzsche, many centuries later, called *amor fati* (love for one's destiny). It is a question of conquering the two evils which, in the eyes of the Greeks, were the present and the future and which Spinoza, in his *Ethica* (1677), defines as *adfecti tristi* (sad emotions).

The ideal figure in this vision is Ulysses in the *Odyssey*. His wanderings after the Trojan War consist in his "going home" to his *natural place*, as Aristotle calls it (Ferry, 1996, 2008). To keep him with her, the goddess Calypso offered him immortality and eternal youth, but Ulysses chose to remain a mortal and return to Ithaca, preferring a successful life as a mortal to an unsuccessful one as immortal. The Greek tradition, as distinct from the Christian, is not very interested in immortality or in an eternal life of salvation: human life serves to demonstrate one's capacities while at the same time recognizing one's limitations. Its aim is not immortality but the struggle to accept the human condition and to live a good life. Each one has one's *natural place* within the *Cosmos*, as every organ has its place within an organism, which can function only if each organ functions and is collocated in its correct position with respect to all the others. When there is dispersion, as happened to Ulysses, it becomes necessary to recover the place which has been lost to re-establish cosmic order. According to Stoic literature Ulysses desires a harmonious life, which is possible only in his natural place, Ithaca, and that is why he rejects Calypso's alluring proposals when she invites him to stay on the enchanting island of Ogygia.

The two messages inherited from mythology and secularised by Greek philosophy define three essential tasks concerning theory (i.e. *Logos, abstract thought, positive thought* independent of any form of mythical or supernatural reality), mortality (aristocratic, which will be explained later on) and the spiritual sphere (the doctrine of salvation and a good life). With regard to these three themes the three great secularising breaks of Christianity will come about: their definition and analysis can be postponed to the following pages.

From *Logos* to Christianity

Greek Stoic philosophy's *Logos*, which for five centuries represented the *Theion* (divine) and the *Cosmos*, soon ran up against a second secularisation when Christianity substituted the *Logos-Man*, Jesus, for the abstract *Logos* of Aristotle and the Stoics. On the theoretical level this constituted a double revolution: first, the *Theion* (divine) was no longer an abstract principle but a person; second, the way to get to know him was not through reason but through faith. Greek philosophy's *Theion*, which, as we have seen, was *Logos* plus *Cosmos*, became in Christianity the divine-humanity of the Messiah. The imposition of the Christian vision was the second great secularisation, which we may define as the "humanisation of the divine". According to Luc Ferry, it was a triple rupture: *theological*, *ethical* and *spiritual*. We shall follow the French philosopher's path as outlined in his work *L'Homme-Dieu* (Ferry, 1996).

Theological rupture: The divine is no longer cosmic order but a person

The first rupture introduced by nascent Christianity was a new concept of the divine, no longer understood (as by the Stoics) as cosmic structure and harmony but as God made man. Therefore God is no longer cosmic order but a person with whom one can have a relationship through faith (rather than through knowledge). According to the Stoics, man must accept his destiny as it is because it corresponds with existing cosmic order. The divine is fused with the order of the world, with destiny, with an impersonal reality. The Stoic ideal is to become an impersonal fragment of a cosmic eternity. But in Christianity the divine is fused with a particular human being who is also God, speaks to his disciples and promises immortality. One's relationship with God becomes a personal relationship, and Providence becomes a form of benevolence on the part of God towards creatures.

The opening sentence of Saint John's Gospel – written in Greek, the language of the Roman imperial East and of philosophy in general – presents this new definition of divinity: "In the beginning was the Word [Logos], and the Word was with God, and the Word was God". Verse 14 continues: "And the Word was made flesh, and dwelt among us". The metaphor of flesh was incomprehensible to the Stoics when referred to the *Theion*, which was no longer anonymous cosmic order but a person, the Man-God who speaks to creatures and saves the world. It is the "death of philosophy" because, differently from the Greek tradition, in Christianity the divine is grasped by faith, not through reason. Although philosophy was deprived of its essential role, it continued to exist but remained at the service of religion until the third secularisation of Humanism. It became that complex of methods and content today known as Scholasticism, devoted to the analysis of notions, having lost its original function of teaching how to live a good life. In the same years as Saint John was drawing up his Gospel, Saint Paul wrote his first Epistle to the Corinthians:

> For the Jews require a sign, and the Greeks seek after wisdom:
> But we preach Christ crucified, unto the Jews a stumblingblock, and unto the Greeks foolishness;
> But unto them which are called, both Jews and Greeks, Christ the power of God, and the wisdom of God.
> Because the foolishness of God is wiser than men; and the weakness of God is stronger than men.
> (1 Corinthians 1: 22–25)[4]

Ethical rupture: All individuals are equal

The theological rupture also had an effect on the moral plane. Christianity was the carrier of a vision of relationships among people which contradicted the three main constitutive principles of aristocratic-elitist Greek morality. We find these data in the writings of Saint Justin Martyr, a Stoic philosopher who converted to Christianity and was put to death during the reign of the Stoic emperor Marcus Aurelius.

Firstly, according to Stoic morality, some people are by nature more talented and gifted than others. This aristocratic view is based on the idea that the moral, political and juridical order should mirror the natural hierarchy of beings. The right city is one which reflects the natural order of individuals, placing the more talented in positions of power. Plato's position in the past was analogous. He felt the social hierarchy should correspond with the hierarchy of the human body: intelligence, reason (*nous*) – the quality of philosophers – is higher up; courage (*thymos*), which in the Greek conception corresponds with the diaphragm, is in the middle – like the warriors who defend the walls of the *polis*; and then there are baser desires (*epithymia*) centred lower down, in the stomach – like the artisans and workers who satisfy the material needs of the social body. There is thus a hierarchy of moral dignity analogous to the anatomical hierarchy. Contrary to this Stoic vision, Christian morality is based rather on the struggle against natural inequalities and involvement in helping the weak.

Secondly, virtue for the Greeks did not consist in struggling against nature but in realising a well-endowed aristocratic nature. The virtuous are those who possess excellent gifts and know how to use them (perfection, even according to Aristotle, consisted in passing from potential to action, from *dynamis* to *energeia*). Here, too, Christian morality is quite different from the Stoic because of its imperative of opposing every form of natural inequality. Virtue is identified with the struggle against everything which is unequal by nature.

Thirdly, for the Greeks the aim of things is inscribed in nature; the ideal is to follow what is written in the nature of things. Nature is the principle of movement, and all that is required of human beings is to stay in (or return to) their places. This is the story of Ulysses, far from home because of the war and then all intent on returning to his natural abode. This is where Christian morality diverges most from the Stoic, particularly because of its view of equality among all individuals. Although nature produces different creatures, each is free to achieve equality. In accordance with Christian morality, based on freedom rather than nature, virtue consists in the transformation of the natural world. The conclusion is that a natural hierarchy of individual gifts does not found a political hierarchy. On the contrary, the nobility of politics is called upon to correct the injustice and inequality inherent in nature. Consequently, for the Christian message, the ideal society is not one which imitates nature in its inequalities but one which pursues the good of all. Here we catch the first glimpses of modernity and democratic societies.

Spiritual rupture: A doctrine of salvation and of living a good life

Christianity introduces a new doctrine of salvation, of living a good life. These themes already existed in Greek philosophy, but with Christianity they acquired added attraction, which helps to explain why they have lasted so long. If the Stoic divine was anonymous, fused with the order and harmony of the universe, the Christian God was concerned with every creature and promised immortality. In this way too, the idea of love and attachment to creatures changes. Above all the concepts of health and salvation – today called spirituality – changed by becoming personal experience in both form and content. Humanisation of the divine and divinisation of the human meet – concludes Ferry – giving rise, however, to misunderstanding in various areas.

This is the Christian perspective which fascinated Justin to the extent that he converted to the religion. The tale is told in his *Apologies* and especially in the proceedings of the trial against him and his disciples. There we find the reasons for the conflict between Stoic philosophy and nascent Christianity concerning the statute of the divine, *Logos* transformed into man and the struggle to overcome natural inequalities. Justin, who lived in the second century, was as we have seen a respected Stoic philosopher before converting to Christianity. After his conversion he wrote two *Apologies* in defence of Christians: the first was addressed to the emperor Antoninus Pius and the second to Marcus Aurelius. There the philosopher talks about the fascination of the *Logos* being made "flesh" and salvation no longer seen as blind providence but as a personal relationship with God made man. He wrote that the Stoic God was blind, without conscience, whereas the Christian God was interested in each one of us, promising us eternity and love. Thus also the attitude towards love and attachment to creatures – which the Stoics had resisted – changed. From the Christian point of view, one's loved one is saved, love being stronger than death, because after death people who have been separated are reunited. So profane did the Christian *divine-humanity* idea appear that – albeit wise and enlightened – the emperor Marcus Aurelius had Justin and his disciples put to death. Apart from his *Apologies*, the most serious charge levelled against Justin was a text containing a dialogue between him and the rabbi Trypho of Ephesus. The theme of their debate was whether the *Theion* should be identified with cosmic order or with a person who was together human and divine. The Christian answer was too radical for Marcus Aurelius's circle (which included the prefect who condemned Justin) and was fatal for the Stoic philosopher turned Christian.

Concluding this short overview of the second secularisation (from Greek philosophy to Christianity), it is not possible to ignore the profound theoretical, ethical and spiritual fractures which it produced. Such deep, lasting fractures that in the West today one cannot describe oneself as non-Christian – at least as regards the idea of the person, equality of rights, work, salvation and a well-lived life.

Modernity and scientific autonomy

The third secularisation, involving the evolution of Western societies from the fourteenth century onwards, is the one most studied in social sciences, starting with Max Weber.[5] The most convincing sociological literature is that which considers this third secularisation as an effect, on the religious plane, of a general functional differentiation throughout Western society which specialised the skills of already-existing subsystems (family, school, economics, politics, care, religion and culture) and created new ones, these too specialised (Gilli, 2016: 80 ff.). Every subsystem had to concentrate on its own functions, giving up various other functions which had previously belonged to its area of responsibility. Consider, for example, how many functions and responsibilities the traditional family had to renounce, becoming a nuclear family with two working parents. And it is this concurrence of multiple subsystems, each with its own specific functions, which represents the complexity of contemporary society. For the subsystems which in the past had had widespread competences it meant both a loss of importance (symbolic and real, individual and collective) and competitive, conflictual confrontation with other subsystems.

For the religious subsystem this delimitation of responsibilities implied significant effects, perhaps even greater than those suffered by the family, which also witnessed a severe reduction of its responsibilities. In traditional society it was the religious subsystem which gave shape, rules and times to economic, social and cultural activities. From the womb to the tomb it was religion which endowed meaning and sense on individuals' lifestyles, sometimes transforming even the most profane activities into sacraments and rituals. The hours of the day, from dawn to dusk, were marked by sacred signs and sounds. Even the times of the year followed a liturgical calendar with its seasons, its prohibitions and its festivals. Working practices obeyed a series of religious rules and regulations. And rituals conferred importance and sacrality upon all things public and private (eating, partying, commemorating anniversaries) as well as "rites of passage" (births, marriages, illness, death). Willy-nilly religion interacted with every area of the lives of believers and non-believers alike, and everybody had to recognize that it was fundamental for producing social cohesion and identity within communities (Heller, 1970: Part II).

The secularisation which followed upon Western scientific development deprived religion of many of its functions and responsibilities, rendering civil society autonomous, independent and separated from the *sacred*. And this is precisely contemporary *secular society* which, during its long-lasting history, has witnessed the evolution of multiple processes of *disenchantment* of the world, to use the language of Max Weber. The reality in front of our eyes is that contemporary societies are by now definitively secular in their private and public institutions. As Peter Berger writes, referring to religious America and lay Europe:

> What has really happened is that religious communities have survived and even prospered to the extent that they have not attempted to adapt to the supposed needs of a secularised world. Modernity, for perfectly understandable reasons, sabotages all the old certainties; and uncertainty is a condition which many people find it hard to endure. Therefore, every (not only religious) movement which promises to supply or renew certainties has to meet the challenge of an open market.
> (Berger, 1999: 3 [our translation])

This observation seems to contradict the thesis of those who foresaw for our age not only quantitative *micro-secularisation* (that of individual beliefs) or *meso-secularisation* (that of individual practices) but also qualitative *macro-secularisation* (that of the irrelevance of religion, which no longer inspires a people's institutions, laws or culture). In reality today's environment is one where religions are compared, often conflictually, with the social and political forces of the majority. Sometimes they challenge the legitimacy and autonomy of primary secular spheres such as the state and the market economy. "What's at stake is the definition of modern borders between the public and private spheres, between the system and the living world, between legality and morality, between the individual and society, among the family, civil society and the state, among nations, states, civilisations and the global system" (Casanova, 2000: 12 [our translation]).

Let us examine more in detail the effects of secularisation on spiritualities, which in some sense represented a subsystem of every religion. The first point is that secularisation did not cause spiritualities to disappear, although it transformed many of their traditional expressions. The second is that this transformation takes place on the levels both of structure, relative to the various systems and subsystems, and of individuals' personalities, value systems and lifestyles. A lot of research testifies that secularisation had a greater effect on relations between believers and church institutions than on the vitality of popular religiosities or on new spiritualities. So the principle – consequent upon a hyper-integrated, total view of society – that if society is secularised so then are all its individuals equally secularised is not valid. The third point useful for explaining the evident qualitative and quantitative transformations of contemporary spiritualities is the evolution experienced by communities such as Catholic parishes where once upon a time many of the spiritualities were born and located. Indeed it is parochial communities which, in the general secularisation process, have undergone radical modifications. For demographic, urbanisation and labour-organization reasons, today they have seen their function as *communities of belonging* disappear. Parishes great and small have lost their historical inhabitants who, all their lives, considered them as points of reference, sharing their views of the world and civil and religious practices.

Autonomy of lifestyles

What has been written above about the third secularisation is but a thumbnail sketch of the huge body of work which has been done is social sciences in Weber's wake. But what further transformations have involved religions and individuals' spiritual experiences from the 1960s to today? The hypothesis here is that a fourth secularisation has been set in motion. Whereas the third secularisation initiated the separation of religion from various (economic, juridical, political, cultural and daily life) spheres of society, today it is everyday life which is pursuing autonomous development through the liberalisation of lifestyles.

With the fourth secularisation we are witnessing the fulfilment of Hugo Grotius's 1625 principle *etsi deus non daretur* (as if God did not exist), which could today be joined by the formula *etsi communitas non daretur* (as if the community did not exist). In the religious field too, modernity has rarefied links with churches and tradition. Today the fourth secularisation has further slackened bonds, traditions and compulsory rites. The autonomy of lifestyles does not herald the death of the religious but rather the tendency of the individual to design one's own life project and new spiritual profiles which attract because of their free nature and their personalised, horizontal practices. These lifestyles chosen individually are composite, eclectic, and their practices are based mainly on interpersonal relations with other religious environments and individuals, with which/whom the individual might never enter into direct contact, being acquainted with them virtually through social media and networks. This is the life condition which also weakens religious practices and behaviour inherited at birth. As a general rule, such lifestyles configure spiritualities composed of individuals who have chosen them on the basis of needs, interests and personal sensibility.

The fourth secularisation also secularises religious practices, making them independent from religions and collocating them with styles of life though which individuals communicate – to themselves and to others – who they are, who they think they resemble and from whom they would like to distinguish themselves, defining a unitary sense for their existence and behaviour. Lifestyles are a particular feature of today's society where it is often not values, ideologies or even social position which explain people's behaviour but rather tastes, sensibility, personal interests and fashionable trends.

Today, two millennia after the beginning of Christianity, we have the *secular condition*, the final effect of the secularisation process, which is enveloping the planet in a new vision of life, sufficient unto itself, by indicating lifestyles and an individual and collective sense of life. The gods, devils, celestial beings and the institutions representing them have been overcome. Things of the past remain in books – and of course in people's hearts – while daily life and lifestyles autonomously go their own way. A sign of this is irritation with rituals and repeated, formalised practices (Calasso, 2017). Lifestyles have precedence in every situation and environment: *rituals, no*; *autonomous lifestyles, yes*. Advertising is the *zeitgeist* of this atmosphere, an essential condition for "being there", and because "everybody sees me".

In the *secular condition* images of a distant God leave space for fractal spiritualities, new religions, and well-being technologies and markets. The divine becomes lived corporeality, that is, capable of releasing intellectual, dissipating and transforming energy. The very soul of secular society is exposed: it had already been glimpsed by the sociologist Émile Durkheim, who said that in order to ensure social cohesion it was no longer enough to deify kings and great leaders – as happened in the past – but it was necessary to deify society itself (Durkheim, 1964). Social cohesion becomes a divine substance circulating in the social body. Society itself – sometimes the market – is for its members what God once was for the faithful.

In this context what may be termed "fractal religious forms" take shape. A fractal, understood as a structure which does not change although differentiating itself with many modalities, might appear as a rare artificial construction. But the fact is that it is common in nature: examples are the arrangement of the branches of a tree, the configuration of a cauliflower, the distribution of pulmonary cells, the surface of clouds, a river's course, the structure of the galaxies, a bolt of lightning and the ramifications of an ion deposited in an electrolytic process. The fractal form is potent not only in the language of mathematics (where it is much more common than the circle or the square) but equally in understanding nature and applied to teleological sciences.

In the religious field the fractal is the multiplication of forms, both the multiplication of religious institutions (churches, sects, movements, online sites) and the multiplication of sensibilities, interests and spiritualities. Recently these last have taken shape autonomously outside religions, adapting to individuals' needs for completion, healing and enlightenment: the myths and narratives which gave rise to these are weak or have disappeared, especially in their transcendent dimension. Spiritualities are sometimes *orphaned*, lacking much efficaciousness. All of this happens in a contemporary context which is witnessing the uprooting of the traditional bases of sense, e.g. the ideologies of the past. More and more people see themselves as *orphan*s of every social, cultural and religious past, for which reason they build a spiritual identity and lifestyles for their existence. New spiritual practices and new visions of the world are formed; other religious alphabets are tried out; ancient texts and masters are discovered. In all of this spiritualities (even more than religions) are the key to interpreting the profound transformations which are still being caused by secularisation in both the private and public spheres. *Inertia of belonging*, which explains the continuity of religions, does not exist in spiritualities. Even the market has observed this fact, opening up a specific field devoted to spiritual services, tracking people in their daily lives, their education, their workplaces, their holiday resorts and the places where they go to seek physical and interior wellbeing.

It is well to remember that *homo saecularis* did not need to wait for current sociological investigations in order to take up residence in the fourth secularisation. We can find him already present in historical descriptions of mediaeval man in his daily life – in the squares, in the theatres, in taverns and in brothels. Today, on the other hand, *homo saecularis* is convinced that he lives normally since he himself has become a perfect *homme moyen*. *Homo saecularis* today is a refined, complex product of historical evolution and religious transformation, so unexpected that not even he knows what he is or what will be the future of his world.

Thus with the loss of relevance of organized historical religions, the religious has not been extinguished, but *homo saecularis*'s sensibilities and needs are being transformed, with all the importance he attributes to freedom of choice and change experimented and substituted in ways which were unthought of in traditional societies. Max Weber had already foreseen it when he wrote that it was the disenchantment of the world, from the beginning of the fourteenth century onwards, that changed the traditional religious into secular forms, that is to say independent from the defined dogmatic contents and restrictions of historical religions. Sometimes it is in this context that we find a humanist secularity which on one hand contains religious groups functioning as social-welfare agencies and, on the other, secular individuals who act like ecclesiastical ministers of solidarity. In this case humanist secularisms are not formed after or against religions but are themselves religious forms in planetary expansion, capable of embracing different religions, movements and trends. French *laïcité* is one form of humanist secularism which in many ways reveals itself in competition with traditional religions (Calasso, 2017).

Since the *secular condition* has always existed, what is new? What is new is its *normality* – its being the condition of the *homme moyen*, the *average man*. The *secular condition* is that expressed by an interviewee in a recent survey who replied, "*I am neither a believer nor an atheist – I am a normal person*". The traditional religious person had certain religious obligations and duties. *Homo saecularis* lives for himself, almost as if he owed nothing to anybody. Literature described him long before social sciences did. It is inevitable that in this kind of life uncertainty, alternation and the effort of choosing will continue to be a source of unease for contemporary man. Normality substitutes the norms of historical religions. But the secular condition does not aim at challenging or – even less – substituting traditional religious identities. The new principle is *belonging without believing*, inverting the well-known *believing without belonging*. Believing and participating autonomously and in a personalised way does not prevent one from still remaining within a historical-religious tradition. But everything – including anxiety and uncertainty – is personal, individualised.

All research into contemporary atheism testifies to the difficulty of finding people who declare themselves to be atheists, considering the word excessive, too final. "Agnostic" is preferred, as is "seeking" and – more recently – "ana-theist". SBNR (*spiritual but not religious*) is the most widespread profile, the prevalent identity of the secular condition. Intolerant of all organized religion, the *spiritual but not religious* are sensible of a more fluid spiritual dimension than the religious. The *milieux* in which they immerse themselves, finding there "the beyond" and the transcendent, are the aesthetic dimension of the landscape, of music, of painting and, lastly, humanitarian causes. In this they are "pilgrims of the absolute", consciously seeking: that is why they reject "the religious", which is precisely the home where residents and natives of a religion live.

Modernity, from the advent of Protestantism onwards, has rarefied the vertical links in the religious field with traditions and churches.

> Protestantism seems to dilute the content of religious discourse until it expels it altogether, until the faithful subject is precipitated, as in the case of the Quakers, into an atmosphere of abyssal rarefaction with no toeholds. If on one hand it protects the centre of the religious hemisphere from every human mark, leaving the empty shadow of transcendence camping there, on the other it also erodes ritual, inventing a God who speaks not to collectives but to individuals. It is Protestantism which is the true religion of modernity, the one which was born and nurtured by the invention of human distinctiveness at the ending of the Middle Ages.
>
> (Leone, 2014: 23 [our translation]).

Modernity, at the ending of the Middle Ages, initiated the religion – or religiosity, when referring to individuals – of human distinctiveness and of the passage from "God" to "I". Even when the religious sense is experienced collectively, the community is a rarefied social form, like different individualities vibrating together or paradoxically sharing the same taste for silence and solitude. They are collective forms of spiritual happenings without transcendence, of private temples, of new sacred idols, which fill the religious-sense gap left over from vertical bonds and traditions. At the conclusion of his volume about digital spirituality, the semiologist Leone describes one such new collective ritual – applause:

> One cannot but be moved by a humanity which applauds death. The applause is certainly not for the deceased, for the feats which s/he may have carried out in life and will now be blocked for him/her. No, the crowd is celebrating itself with its applause, as if to say well done, as if to express an explosion of satisfaction at a dancer's successful pirouette, or a jazz musician's acrobatic improvisation.
>
> (ibid.: 46 [our translation]).

Applause is a new form of commonality; but it is directed at oneself and the group which, at certain moments, frees itself from the fragmentation of digital narcissism to draw close together in the face of that infinite elsewhere called death.

What, then, is religious sense in the *secular* age? International literature has identified four main drivers of the transformations in progress in the religious field in advanced modernity: de-institutionalisation, de-personalisation, the emersion of new social forms of the religious, and the multiplication of spiritualities (Nesti, 1985; Cipriani, 1988; Lerat and Rigal-Cellard, 2000; Campiche, 2004; Ammerman, 2007; Beck, 2008; Baumann and Stolz, 2009; Berger, Davie, and Fokas, 2008; Garelli, Guizzardi, and Pace, 2003; Turner, 2011; Gorski, Kyuman Kim, Torpey, and VanAntwerpen, 2012; Norris and Inglehart, 2004; MacKian, 2012; Gauthier and Martikainen, 2013; Obadia, 2013; Giordan and Pace, 2014; Stolz, Könemann, Schneuwly Purdie, Englberger, and Krüggeler, 2015). Based on these driving factors, this section puts forward the hypothesis that the fourth secularisation consists in the autonomy of lifestyles and, more generally, of daily life.

The drivers of the fourth secularisation

First of all, as we have seen above, there is a de-institutionalisation of religious style, its passage from the institutional sphere to the subjective sphere. There is a weakening of traditional socialisation processes in the new generations, by means of which processes, whether directly or indirectly, religious institutions managed to transmit their cultural and lifestyle models. It is a very different context from that in which a concentricity of belongings deriving from total adherence to a territorial community (parish, town, neighbourhood) was in itself educational. Experience of the plurality of social worlds characteristic of the secular age makes the institutional sphere irrelevant in all spheres, including the religious, so that an individual's personal experiences acquire more weight and reality than institutional ones – they acquire today a legitimacy, recognition and credibility to an extent which would have been unthinkable in traditional society. The choice and constructions of one's spirituality now belong to the category of life-projects to be built individually – along with education, work and family.

The individual – who today has become a *multiple I* varying in time and identifying with her/his spirituality in different ways according to the daily environments s/he frequents – is led to follow changing, successive choices even in the spiritual field. In Chapter 2 we saw the two concepts of individualisation and differentiation which Simmel identified as the cornerstones of every – individual and collective – social evolution (Simmel, 1890). Both respond to the need to affirm one's personality through qualitative differentiation which has the function of attracting the attention of the group to which one belongs. Individualisation and differentiation with respect to other members of the group are among the main motivations soliciting and determining individuals' action. Thus there is a *differentiated subjectivity* in the religious field too, almost as if to avoid the individual's uniqueness becoming lost in objectified forms. Therefore, with the multiplication of lifestyles in horizontal societies, even in the religious field there is a passage from unitary spirituality (typical of institutions) to plural spirituality (typical of subjects). Spiritualities multiply, then, in the same way as lifestyles, under the impulse of individual desire to differentiate oneself also in the field of religious identity.

A lifestyle, as we have just seen, is objectified and multiplies, making itself available to whomsoever adopts it, using it in his/her own way and connoting it with personal meanings and functions regardless of its original axiological dimension. In this personalisation process, the number of individuals and spiritualities with no fixed religious status increases. This does not, however, herald the end of the spiritual dimension but rather the individual tendency to construct one's own spiritual-life project. The dissolution of a single subject profile leads to interpreting spiritual identity as an arena of possibilities and limitations which belong contemporaneously to several different worlds. The emphasis placed on the self and its authenticity is an integral part of secular spiritualities where the nexus between spiritual and physical health is seen in one of most recurrent greetings (i.e. "prayers"): Take care of yourself! Health and salvation are often intertwined, creating a state of overall wellbeing where there is no longer a clear distinction between the physical and spiritual dimensions. The basis is a set of needs relating to diet, health and interpersonal relations from which grows a novel therapeutic and spiritual network.

The second driving force behind advanced modernity is the personalisation of belief.

> Perceiving more weakly the bond of obedience towards traditional religious authorities, and seeing freedom of choice socially recognized, legitimated and often even invoked, the individual has the power – if not the duty – to choose not only among a selection of possible religious proposals which includes predefined traditions, doctrines and religious organizations, but also among specific beliefs and elements of faith which can potentially be de-contextualised from the tradition and organization within which they were developed.
>
> (Genova, 2016: 11 [our translation])

There is a growing tendency towards free composition of the elements of one's own lifestyle (Roof, 1993, 1999, 2003). This personal generativity of styles did not, however, impede the adoption of new beliefs and practices or the attribution to them of precise meaning coming about through collective modalities shared with others. This is the collective – albeit informal – dimension of lifestyles. Various names have been given to such empowerment of religious styles: religious DIY, *à la carte* religion, religious patchwork, New Age religiosity, designer religion, super-individualism. The different definitions indicate that set of practices (behaviour, beliefs, experiences, rituals, knowledge, reading) which today individuals and groups cultivate with greater freedom than in the past. It is the phenomenon by which the idea of the religious "free market" of symbolic good joins the idea of utilitaristic individual behaviour. It is advanced modernity which creates a religious individual of this kind: a subject who composes at the same time, and freely, social cohesion and autonomy, continuity and discontinuity with respect to the bonds of tradition and the community; in other words, who creates the religious individual without a rigidly normative morality or faith. One of the religious profiles emerging from recent research is that of "I'm a believer, but in my own way". In the Catholic Church this has meant faithful who participate in religious functions related to family life, perhaps go on a pilgrimage or join in festivities in honour of a saint, but then autonomously structure their behaviour. The final result, for all religions, is the multiplication of religious lifestyles even within the religions themselves. In traditional societies there was only one religious lifestyle: that indicated by the legitimate authority; but today lifestyles of belief, practice and recognizing certain moral duties depend increasingly upon individual choices. What had already happened in the great crisis of Greek myths has cropped up again: the Gods,

48 The fourth secularisation

made by men in their own image and adored by them, had become more useful for explaining the big questions such as pain, death and the future than for guiding people's daily lives. This caused the fragility of those Gods as truly autonomous entities.

A third driving force behind the fourth secularisation has to do with new social forms in the religious sphere. The de-institutionalisation and personalisation of which we have spoken contribute to the rise of new modalities of religious sharing, or new horizontally produced lifestyles, such as fashions and trends (Roof, 1999; Fuller, 2001; Usunier and Stolz, 2014). From them spring religious beliefs and practices – lifestyles – resulting more from interaction and the social context than from traditional agencies of religious socialisation. This happens also in churches, such as the Catholic, where the percentage of members is much higher than those who adopt personalised lifestyles "selected" from different religious traditions which do not necessarily provoke conversion or close identification but rather interest and exploration. Such horizontally formed lifestyles constituted of interpersonal relations indicate:

> . . . the progressive erosion not so much of the collective dimension of the religious – albeit partially weaker than in the past – as primarily of its institutionalised declension, a growing centrality of the individual, and its more liberal and reflective approach to belief, even in collective experiences.
>
> (Genova, 2016: 14 [our translation])

At the heart of this is the element, typical of modernity, of life-*chances*, opportunities, and the near-duty of choosing personally. *Styles*, rather than *the* style, are the most functional form in such a context. If this tendency were to be unstoppable, we would witness the weakening of traditional bonds and a situation of anomy, with a lack of normative elements shared by all and the multiplication of personal choices; neither indifference nor silence towards religions but rather fragmentation of the great narratives and of religious traditions. The dogmas of ideological atheism having been broken up, the fourth secularisation multiplies subjective visions and religious *loisirs*. As a hermeneutic background available to everybody, there is a multiplication of spiritual visions within which individual and collective life events can be collocated. The result is a personal religion which the sociologist Robert Bellah has defined as *Sheilaism*, from the name (Sheila) of a woman whom he interviewed: there are as many religions as there are inhabitants on Planet Earth (Bellah, 1985: 180 ff.). As to the effective liberty of choice of these multiple personal experiences, one cannot recognize in them excessive autonomy. Even these new believers are much more hetero-directed than they themselves may think. Consumer-society markets tell them what they should consume, even in the religious field; and they do not always convincingly resist market temptations.

Particular interest is shown today in the religious lifestyle, typical of contemporary religiosity, which has been defined as *practising without believing*. It is the lifestyle which can be seen in those experiences which develop essentially from individual adoption of multiple religious practices not deriving any more – as in the past – from beliefs, but horizontally through observation and imitation of others. Yet these practices are nonetheless endowed with unitary sense in the eyes of whoever adopts them and can be shared with greater or smaller collectivities. In some cases (but only afterwards) they may be accompanied by a sharing of doctrinal elements, that is, of beliefs.

In the religious sphere too, research documents the multiplication of trends and individual lifestyles based on the choice of one's own experiences and practices, recomposed into new symbolic alphabets – personal or collective liturgies – which celebrate the creativity of religious individuals or groups (Berzano and Genova, 2010; Palmisano, 2016; Berzano, 2017). Analogous to what happens in the consumer society, we can say that in the religious field there is a passage from status symbols to style symbols, by means of which also religious practices are separated from their roles as indicators of class or ascribed belonging, attaining an entirely communicative dimension. Research into new youth spiritualities increasingly indicates the affirmation of these lifestyles based on expressive and emotive affinity. They are "bosom" spiritualities based on solidarity and collective narcissism. A culture founded on imagery and the hyper-production of communications free from reference to authority follows upon the loss of narratives with a purpose and general normative systems. This anthropological mutation gives rise to a new social actor who favours aesthetic knowledge, artistic knowledge and expressive knowledge. It is a dimension of the fourth secularisation: the normalisation of the aesthetic, which permits styles of life to be considered art and allows one to approach an aesthetic object with an autonomous, amused attitude. If the spiritual dimension does not belong to the material plane, then it should be sought in every heart.

The fourth guiding principle is the multiplication of new spiritualities where we can find *immanent transcendence* in the Durkheim tradition. This transcendental vision contains both the original meaning of religion as an experience of *re-ligare* (tie again) and as a bond/relationship between the self and the *beyond*, and as that of *re-legere* (re-read, reinterpret) as translating the everyday into *more* and as an infinite interpretation/translation of the human into the divine and the divine into the human. This gives rise to interest in broadening the concept of spirituality so as to include its new forms.

One of these is *Godless spirituality*, interpretations of life and sets of practices which are no longer anchored to prevalently metaphysical thought but where transcendental signs are still represented by a global sense given to life, by the nostalgia of hope, by totalising I-You encounters, by analysis of the ethical imperative, by freedom from alienation and by each individual's feeling of interior solitude. These spiritualities are those where the *different* (i.e. the divine) introduces transcendental elements into the *similar* (i.e. the everyday). This is nothing new. At the beginning of the twentieth century, at the heart of modernity, Georg Simmel introduced an analogous form to identify the "non-church religious": "religiosity" characterized by a maximum degree of independence from every religious tradition, partly because it always precedes it. Simmel's "religiosity" is the state in which one finds oneself when one is willing to believe in – and experience – mystery. His conclusion is the opposite of the usual one that new religiosities grow out of religion.

> Just as knowledge does not create causality but causality creates knowledge, in the same way religion does not create religiousness but religiousness creates religion. Fate – as known by mankind in the context of a certain internal state of mind – decrees agitation of relationships, meanings and feelings which are not yet in themselves religion. Their reality content has nothing to do with it – even for those souls who are differently disposed, but freed from this reality (and in some way hardened by their pervading religiosity) they thus create for themselves a realm of the objective, thereby achieving 'religion', which here means the objective world of faith.
>
> (Simmel, 1992: 197 [our translation])

With the multiplication of forms of religiosity described by Simmel, we see secular society "invading the pitch" of religious environments. Everything indicates a condition where "the sacred face" – which once contained all of society and the lives of individuals – is disappearing. The spiritualities to which this work refers have many analogies with Simmel's concept of religiosity. New spiritualities, too, are independent of religions. The controlling power which churches exercised over spiritual forms considered too free, individual and experiential is also disappearing. As they advance, even the idea of God becomes polymorphous in its many views and representations: Christianity's personal being, a purely spiritual and impersonal deity, mysticism's interior God, Romain Rolland's and Sigmund Freud's "oceanic feeling" and the many multiple images of the New Age universe. In this polysemy of the sense of "God" can be included that of the unknown, the unspeakable, the impersonal, mystical, interior, purely spiritual being.

God becomes a common name, a poetic term, a rhetorical metaphor to indicate energy, momentum, a dream, mystery. None of this means necessarily desacralisation or a new interpretation of age-old pantheism or the animism of archaic religions. Rather than *avatars* of ancient religions, these new spiritualities anticipate a different sensibility and interest – with or without traditional religions' image of the typical God.

In traditional spiritualities too, we find linguistic variations in the names of God: transcendence, divine, divinity, Spirit. Saint Bernard of Clairvaux, monk and Doctor of the Catholic Church, wrote in a twelfth-century sermon about the *Canticle of Canticles*: "We seek that which the eye cannot see, that which the ear cannot hear, that which the heart has not tasted. Whatever that is, it is what attracts us and what we are seeking" (Bernard de Clairvaux, 1663: 227 [our translation]). And the French writer-ethnographer Victor Segalen (1878–1919) wrote: "I pay attention to what has not yet been said. I submit to what has not yet been promulgated. I am subject to what does not yet exist" (Segalen, 1973: 37 [our translation]).

This analogical interpretation of spirituality and the concept of religion itself can be found in its most radical form in Walter Benjamin's fragment *Kapitalismus als Religion*, where capitalism (rather than a secularised religion, as Max Weber claims) is an essentially religious phenomenon. The German philosopher supports his thesis with four elements: 1) capitalism is "a purely cultural religion, perhaps the most extreme there has ever been"; 2) it is "the celebration of the *without a truce and without mercy* cult", where every day is a holiday; 3) it is "the first example of a cult which does not atone for sin but creates guilt/debt"; and 4) as a religion, capitalism's god must be concealed – man is not allowed to turn to this god except at the zenith of his guilt. In the religious form implying perseverance to the end, the transcendence of God does not disappear, and God himself is not dead but rather included in human destiny (Benjamin, 1996).

Once again it was Benjamin who recognized that this vision of religious blaming/indebtedness found its greatest expression in Nietzsche's philosophy. It may be added that, from Nietzsche onwards, the whole debate about the death of God and traditional theology facilitated the evolution of a precise outline of faith both for those inside the church and those who had left it: a faith which fully tended towards non-religious Christianity, personal religiosity and social engagement. This outline is visible in Emmanuel Lévinas's formula whereby God has given life to a being capable of atheism, able to live in society, according to Hugo Grotius's already-cited words, "as if God did not exist". Such an interpretation has initiated a field of analysis increasingly interested in studying reciprocal spirituality-atheism relations.

In what way does spirituality involve atheism, and how does atheism oblige spirituality to live together with post-secular society? Whereas in the past these relations impoverished both spirituality and atheism, today they re-introduce two important data. The first is the claim that spirituality (as well as religion) is not only a reminder of a primitive past destined to vanish in modernity. This vision of the dissolution of religion, or at least its reduction to one among many simple private functions in complex, differentiated societies, has been short-lived. Charles Wright Mills's forecast of the gradual evolution of a sacred universe and a secular one has turned out to be equally illusory: "Once the world was filled with the sacred – in thought, practice, and institutional form. After the Reformation and the Renaissance, the forces of modernization swept across the globe and secularization, a corollary historical process, loosened the dominance of the sacred. In due course, the sacred shall disappear altogether except, possibly, in the private realm" (Mills, 1959: 32–33).

The second datum is that in the secular society atheism no longer needs to mistake for its adversary a spirituality which is attentive to action and the world's suffering. Such a possibility of a creative, fertile relationship between atheism and spirituality has been proposed by – among others – Raimon Panikkar, strenuous defender of the need to conserve the fecund tension between the *secular I* and the *spiritual I* (Panikkar, 1993). Only secularisation can prevent the sacred from becoming a negation of life, and only a spiritual vision of the world and of life can prevent atheism from becoming fanatical and blind. The sacred and the secular are different poles of life: the former is the pole of finite time and daily life; the latter of infinity, otherness and transcendence. Humankind can embrace both of them.

Further studies of Godless spiritualities can be found in the spirituality-for-the-skeptic disciplinary field and in the *International Journal for the Study of Skepticism* (2010–2013). These analyses started with the publication of Robert Solomon's volume *Spirituality for the Skeptic* (2002), the most significant work concerning naturalised, secular spirituality, attempting to defend the credibility and integrity of secular spirituality as "ontological gratitude". Other scholars (Dawkins, 2006; Dennet, 2006) subsequently developed this view of a secular, atheist world from a perspective which has been defined "hermeneutics of ontological gratitude" (Colledge, 2013). All have tried to dissipate Max Weber's criticism of modernity and its effects of disenchantment and downward levelling, which rob spiritual life of its enchantment and depth. The general thesis of this secular spirituality movement – if such an internally diversified phenomenon may be properly so called – is that every secular spirituality should be capable of taking into consideration not only the sign of gratitude for itself and its own existence but for the entire collective-being context.

In what sense can a spirituality with a great anti-supernatural naturalism contain a strong sense of gratitude? Moreover, is such profound gratitude for life experiences really possible only for those who hold that there is Something or Someone – for example, a divine creator – which fills one with wonderment? According to Richard Dawkins, this ontological gratitude is totally possible in a serious existential reflection, albeit independent of every theistic belief, despite compatibility with the idea of a divine creator (Dawkins, 2006). The same author associates reverence for, and fear of, what contemporary sciences reveal about the surprising complexity and beauty of the cosmos, evoking the possibility of a mystical response to nature – a response which is completely distinct from positive conviction of a supernatural God. More recently Dawkins has claimed that existence itself is something to be grateful for and that gratitude is important even for an evolutive naturalist (Colledge, 2013).

Adopting the *Godless spirituality* concept enables recognition of new forms of spirituality appearing today and gradually expanding. These forms are characterized by being based on the sharing of behaviour and practices repeated over time which, in the eyes of individuals, are not configured as independent of one another but are reciprocally interconnected. This set of practices confers sense on the life of the individual and endows it with a spiritual dimension, but without depending upon the individual's own religion when it is a question of believers. From this point of view traditional relationships among religious affiliation, faith and practices turn out to be much more complex. Recently, in order to interpret contemporary spiritualities, many researchers have adopted the *believing without belonging* formula designed by Grace Davie at the conclusion of a study of the English Anglican Church (Davie, 1994). But in the light of this model, today spiritualities rather of the behaving without believing type seem to be spreading. One can increasingly observe spiritual (and even religious) lifestyles of individuals who adopt a set of practices, endowed with a unitary sense, shared in greater or lesser collectives – to which is added only in some cases, and subsequently, a sharing of doctrinal elements. Practices sometimes develop within organized groups, but in many cases they are individually cultivated. This new form of religion or spirituality is not only particularly difficult to interpret by means of classical analytical tools but also – viewed through these lenses – risks not even being identified as a form of spirituality.

Our proposal here is to interpret such forms as spiritualities in accordance with the definition of lifestyles presented in Chapter 1. The definition is based on a comprehensive model with both spiritual and sociological contents: the former refer to the dimensions of spiritual sensibility, transcendency, inner life, and seeking sense and experience; the latter to the dimensions of practices, sense and meaning, collective distinguishing and sharing, modalities and intensity of involvement, and spirituality's generative elements (Berzano and Genova, 2008, 2015).

Conclusion

This section on the four forms of secularisation started with Greek philosophy, which grew out of the secularisation of the divine presences in mythology by their rational reformulation. Modern humanism, too, and later Descartes's and Hegel's rationalism, emerged from the secularisation of a part of the Christian religion. Kant founded a completely lay morality based not on a religion but on a consideration of the interests of human reason. All great philosophies have been the fruit of the secularisation of a previous religion, to the extent that one cannot understand the great currents of philosophy without first knowing the religions. In the preface to his work *The Dawn of Day* (1881), Nietzsche claimed to be the heir of the Enlightenment and those who had secularised religion, and he declared his desire to continue the work of secularisation, since even the Enlightenment contained its religious structure. One might say that Nietzsche's work found its fulfilment in the religion theorized by Marcel Gauchet and by those who reject religion as heteronomy.

The core element of the fourth secularisation resides in the notion of *sociological horizontality*, which, when applied to society and lifestyles, turns out to be an adequate indicator of the profound transformation involving religious systems too and their members' styles of belief and practice. *Sociological horizontality* concerns religious freedom, the absence of the principle whereby there is only one true religion, the uncoupling of identity and identification.

Horizontal religiosity consists of the disappearance of the conviction that the religion into which we were born is an obligatory inheritance which must not be renounced and the parallel growth of the conviction that even religion is a matter of personal choice. Once it was rare to abandon one's birth religion: at most one no longer practised, or one moved from one kind of spirituality to another – but within the same religion. It was more common to reject one's religion altogether than to choose another one. Today, by contrast, the principle of free choice permits (and, in a certain sense, encourages) freeing oneself at will from one's religion and dedicating oneself to another which gives greater personal satisfaction. The idea of personal choice – which is sometimes really only apparent since there are so many forms of conditioning – is the new existential imperative in education, in work, in affective relations, which is to say in one's identity. And the modality of identity-building may be either *vertical* or *horizontal*. The former is typical of traditional societies where everything depended on conditions at birth; the latter is built little by little on the single individual's choices, never definitive, characterized by constant formation and reflexivity. *Horizontal identity* is the new individualism, of a two-faced nature. On one hand it homogenizes everybody in a single lifestyles market inspired by global culture; on the other, it differentiates groups and individuals by emphasizing multiple ethnic and individual identities. The fourth-secularisation hypothesis is that today horizontal lifestyles are spreading even in the religious sphere as distinct from the traditional (vertical) ones which were reproduced (from above to below) on the basis of the influence of whoever represented constituted authority. Today's lifestyles are more open, freer to establish relationships of equality and above all in constant formation: they have characteristics which Robert J. Lifton (1993) defines as "protean", or incessantly changeable.

Secondly, *horizontal religiosity* is related to the weakening of the conviction that one's own is the only true religion, according to the Catholic theological principle *extra Ecclesiam nulla salus* (outside the Church there is no salvation). This is a theological truth, which was once entrusted exclusively to theologians but which today has disappeared from among ordinary people who are not theologians and belong to the horizontal society and its culture (Stolz, Könemann, Schneuwly Purdie, Englberger, and Krüggeler, 2015). In a pluralist society where an individual lives alongside others, affiliates of different religions with whom one enjoys relations of respect and friendship, it is difficult to think that one's religion is the only one necessary in order to live well. It is easier to believe that there are also other paths to salvation, that everybody may choose the one most amenable to her/his inner peace, so there is no one path for everybody.

The dogmatic principle *extra Ecclesiam nulla salus* has been replaced by that of a thousand roads to salvation which are followed according to personal choice. The globalisation of science and technology has broken down the barriers of space and time which separated individuals and has produced a situation in the modern world defined by Peter Berger as "urbanisation of consciousness": everybody is bombarded by a multiplicity of communications and information (Berger, Berger, and Kellner, 1973: 67). New *media* only intensify this horizontal dimension of society and religions, creating an immediate global culture weakening all traditional forms of trust and reciprocity. The fall of religions' vertical structure and hierarchy also implies for them – in the field of reflexive thought – the loss of a unique metaphysical thought in favour of abstraction processes increasingly dominated by science and technology.

Thus even in the religious sphere serial relations (spending some time in one group, then passing to another) may negatively influence the strength of identification with one's religion, provoking forms of cognitive dissonance between one experience and another. The individual weakens the force of adherence to his/her own group, already directing attention towards the next one. Here we observe the phenomenon termed "circular conversions" for both identities and identifications: for the former it means passing from one religion to another; for the latter, successive interests and references to different religions.

Thirdly, *horizontal religiosity* augments the disjunction between identity and identification. The two concepts are preached by single individuals but can be practised only by collective entities (Berzano, Genova, and Pace, 2005). To the individual, *identity* means the capacity to establish an observable difference between oneself and others, maintaining that differentiation over time. It is detectable only with reference to a set of analogous individuals with whom – qua analogous – one is able to identify. *Identification* means the influence which the individual's identifying with the collective entity exercises upon his/her choices and behaviour; therefore it is possible only with reference to another reality/other realities. In the religious arena too, the process of individual identity-building takes place only with reference to an institutionalised religious form to which one intends to belong; thus identity denotes recognition of that religious form on the basis of which the single believer may speak using *we* instead of *I*.

Research is unanimous in that, in modern societies, forms of identity – even more of identification – of a religious type are increasingly differentiated and that what is being greatly weakened is identification, to the extent that the situation can be described as *strong identity, weak identification* (Berzano, 2005: 13–100). In the present religious context, characterized by a great abundance of possible choices and complex options, interviewees subdivide into a minority who are fully involved in their community (or movement, or group) and a majority who consider *strong identification* as a luxury to which they cannot aspire without excessively renouncing their autonomy. We may point out two dimensions of this identity-identification differentiation: the first regards the increase of pluralism and the multiplication of groups and religious education available, in a context which some have called "the religious market"; and the second concerns the differentiation of choices, interests and religious behavioural styles in the same individual. Based on this double differentiation, one may state that opportunities for developing new forms of identity and identification have never been so numerous as in contemporary societies.

In an environment of increasing pluralism, the religious individual who belongs to diverse social and cultural circles (residential, work, recreational, religious, political) has greater opportunities to establish differences and similarities between oneself and others and to develop consequent identification processes. But these identifications are often based on "weak links"; and developing an identification process with a particular religious group does not (yet) mean assuming its identity so much as intensifying one's interests and seeking new stimuli. It means situating one's religious experience in the area of *loisirs* even though such an identification may significantly influence practices and behaviour. At the same time, however, the possibilities of abandoning or loosening links with one's group increase. Indeed every church and religious group possesses a specific subculture, uses its own linguistic codes, has its own history, and elaborates interests and aims different from those of the others. Participating or taking an interest in different groups means setting up a serial relationship with them, abandoning one to enter another, in a more or less rapid sequence. These, too, are some of the elements modifying relations between identity and identification, as Table 3.1 illustrates:

Table 3.1 Social characteristics of religious identity and identification

Religious identity	Religious identification
Ascribed, obligatory	Acquired, voluntary
Institutionally defined and regulated	Autonomous
Fixed, institutionalised	Modular, fluctuating
Collective, communitarian	Individual
Territorial	Moveable
Permanent	Episodic, linked to events

It should not be concluded that this situation of greater freedom/ autonomy of faith is causing the various denominational identities to disappear. This phenomenology of "believing freely" attains more to identification than to identity-building processes. Even in northern European countries, where Catholic-Protestant exchanges have been more intense, denominational religious identity remains strong because it continues to fulfil other – individual and collective – social functions different from those relating to identification. In the Italian context the Catholic collective identity is still that of the majority, including those who say "All religions are equally true". Denominational religious identities continue to define many social networks even as the truly religious aspects continue to decline. The hold of the Catholic identity in Italy is therefore linked with identity re-affirmation, one could say according to the law of inertia. Thus the principal challenge facing the sociology of religious modernity lies in understanding the double movement of the diminished relevance of institutional religious systems and the "grip" of traditional religious identities. This explains the interest in research aimed at overcoming inadequate theories of secularisation – an effort towards which the present volume hopes to contribute.

Notes

1 "Secularisation" is a modern term, born out of the Napoleonic abrogation of German princes' ecclesiastical privileges – a leftover of the mediaeval opposition between pope and emperor. By now the term has acquired a more general denotation, indicating one of the many "deaths" of God, or rather of a certain model of the divine in Western history. Indeed, the God who dies is always "different". Even the term "agnosticism" applied to Protagoras is totally figurative because it does not fully clarify his conception of the divine.
2 It is high time to elucidate religion's political-institutional function: "Democracy, having reached its *ne plus ultra*, was conservative: it condemned philosophers and sought the backing of religion" (D'Agostini, 2016: 267). Apart anyway from doubts about the democratic qualifications of the government of Athens in the fifth and sixth centuries, it is true that that was also the age of trials for "impiety" (*asébeia*), which, according to Aristotle's definition, is a crime committed against the Gods, demons, or even against the dead, one's parents, the homeland. It was the accusation which Anytus and Meletus levelled at Socrates.
3 In the above-quoted 2016 lecture, Fabrizio D'Agostini noted the curious fact that this did not come about as a result of the Sophists' work so much as of that of the "virtuous" Plato. Only Critias among the Sophists followed to their extreme consequences the possibilities implicit in the objectivisation of religious thought and functionalised it as to the ethics of power, seeing in religion a road to political domination. But only Plato radicalised the phenomenon, systematizing it in his doctrine of the state.
4 The quotation is taken from the King James Version of the Bible (2016).
5 In this context *secularisation* – understood as the economic, social and cultural transformation by which some sectors of society become autonomous from religious institutions – is distinct from both *secularism* (the ideology which absolutises worldly reality, asserting that only the empirical world exists and the divine is merely a mental delusion) and *secularity* (an approach which tries to balance being and non-being, eternity and time, the world and God). A secular state is neither atheist nor a theocracy; it is the government of all (economic, cultural and even religious) differences.

References

Ammerman N. T. (ed.) (2007), *Everyday Religion: Observing Modern Religious Lives*, Oxford University Press, London and New York.
Baumann M., Stolz J. (eds) (2009), *La nouvelle Suisse religieuse. Risques et chances de sa diversité*, Labor et Fides, Genève.
Beck U. (2008), *Der eigene Gott: von der Friedensfähigkeit und dem Gewaltpotential der Religionen*, Verlag der Weltreligionen im Insel Verlag, Frankfurt am Main (Eng. Trans. *A God of One's Own*, Polity Press, Cambridge, 2010).
Bellah R. (ed.) (1985), *Habits of the Heart: Individualism and Commitment in American Life*, University of California Press, Berkeley.
Benjamin W. (1996), "Capitalism as Religion", translated by Rodney Livingston in M. Bullock, M. Jennings (eds), *Selected Writings*, Vol. 1, Harvard University Press, Cambridge, MA: 288–291.

Berger P. L. (1999), "The Desecularization of the World: A Global Overview", in P. L. Berger (ed.), *The Desecularization of the World: Resurgent Religion and World Politics*, Ethics and Public Policy Center-Eerdmans Publishing Company, Washington, DC.
Berger P. L., Berger B., Kellner H. (1973), *The Homeless Mind: Modernization and Consciousness*, Penguin Books, Harmondsworth.
Berger P. L., Davie G., Fokas E. (2008), *Religious America, Secular Europe? A Theme and Variation*, Aldershot, Ashgate.
Bernard de Clairvaux (1663), *Les Sermons de Saint Bernard sur le Cantique des Cantiques* (It. Trans. San Bernardo di Chiaravalle, *Sermoni sul Cantico dei Cantici*, Vivere In, Roma, 1996).
Berzano L. (2005), "Religione a Monreale: tra identità e identificazione", in L. Berzano, P. Zoccatelli (eds), *Identità e identificazione. Il pluralismo religioso nell'entroterra palermitano*, Salvatore Sciascia, Roma: 13–100.
Berzano L. (2017), *Spiritualità. Moltiplicazione delle forme nella società secolare*, Bibliografica, Milano.
Berzano L., Genova C. (2008), *I lifestyles nella partecipazione religiosa*, il Segnalibro, Torino.
Berzano L., Genova C. (2010), *La società delle pratiche orizzontali. Percorsi di ricerca e ipotesi*, EMIL, Bologna.
Berzano L., Genova C. (2015), *Lifestyles and Subcultures: History and a New Perspective*, Routledge, Abingdon and New York.
Berzano L., Genova C., Pace E. (2005), "Credere in libertà", in V. Cesareo (ed.), *Ricomporre la vita. Gli adulti giovani in Italia*, Carocci, Roma: 200–233.
Calasso R. (2017), *L'innominabile attuale*, Adelphi, Milano.
Campiche R. J. (ed.) (2004), *Die zwei Gesichter der Religion. Faszination und Entzauberung*, Theologischer Verlag Zürich AG, Zürich.
Casanova J. (2000), *Oltre la secolarizzazione. Le religioni alla riconquista della sfera pubblica*, il Mulino, Bologna (Original Edition *Public Religions in the Modern World*, The University of Chicago Press, Chicago and London, 1994).
Cipriani R. (1988), *La religione diffusa. Teoria e prassi*, Borla, Roma (Eng. Trans. *Diffused Religion*, Springer Nature, Cham, 2017).
Colledge R. J. (2013), "Secular Spirituality and the Hermeneutics of Ontological Gratitude", *Sophia*, 52, n. 1, Springer Netherlands: 27–43.
D'Agostini F. (2016), *Secolarizzazione della cultura occidentale – V secolo a. C.*, Paper for the *Forme dell'ana-teismo contemporaneo* conference (Palazzo Lascaris, Torino, 1–2 December 2016).
Davie G. (1994), *Religion in Britain Since 1945: Believing Without Belonging*, Blackwell, Oxford and Cambridge, MA.
Dawkins R. (2006), *The God Delusion*, Bantam Books, London.
Dennet D. C. (2006), *Breaking the Spell: Religion as a Natural Phenomenon*, Viking, New York.
Detienne M., Vernant J.-P. (1974), *Les ruses de l'intelligence. La métis des Grecs*, Flammarion, Paris.

Detienne M., Vernant J.-P. (1979), *La cuisine du sacrifice en pays grec*, Gallimard, Paris (Eng. Trans. *The Cuisine of Sacrifice Among the Greeks*, University of Chicago Press, Chicago, 1998).
Durkheim É. (1964), *The Division of Labour in Society*, Free Press, New York.
Ferry L. (1996), *L'Homme-Dieu ou le sens de la vie*, Grasset, Paris (Eng. Trans. *Man Made God: The Meaning of Life*, University of Chicago Press, Chicago, 2002).
Ferry L. (2008), *La sagesse des mythes. Apprendre à vivre*, Plon, Paris (Eng. Trans. *The Wisdom of the Myths*, Harper & Collins, New York, 2014).
Frontisi-Ducroux F., Vernant J.-P. (1997), *Dans l'oeil du miroir*, Éditions Odile Jacob, Paris.
Fuller R. C. (2001), *Spiritual, But Not Religious: Understanding Unchurched America*, Oxford University Press, London and New York.
Garelli F., Guizzardi G., Pace E. (eds) (2003), *Un singolare pluralismo*, il Mulino, Bologna.
Gauthier F., Martikainen T. (2013), *Religion in Consumer Society: Brands, Consumers and Markets*, Ashgate, Farnham and Burlington, VT.
Genova C. (2016), *Oltre il credere. Significati e senso nelle pratiche religiose*, Mimesis, Milano.
Gilli G. A. (2016), *Manuale di ex voto*, Fusta Editore, Saluzzo.
Giordan G., Pace E. (eds) (2014), *Religious Pluralism: Framing Religious Diversity in the Contemporary World*, Springer International Publishing Switzerland, Cham.
Gorski P., Kyuman Kim D., Torpey J., VanAntwerpen J. (eds) (2012), *The Post-Secular in Question: Religion in Contemporary Society*, New York University Press, New York.
Heller A. (1970), *A mindennapi élet*, Akadémiai Kiadó, Budapest (It. Trans. *Sociologia della vita quotidiana*, Pgreco, Milano, 2012; Eng. Trans. *Everyday Life*, Routledge, New York, 1986).
Holy Bible: King James Version (2016), Thomas Nelson Publishers, New York.
Leone M. (2014), *Spiritualità digitale: il senso religioso nell'era della smaterializzazione* (Spiritualità senza Dio, 3), Mimesis, Milano.
Lerat C., Rigal-Cellard B. (eds) (2000), *Les mutations transatlantiques des religions*, PUB, Pessac.
Lifton R. J. (1993), *The Protean Self: Human Resilience in an Age of Fragmentation*, Basic Books, New York.
MacKian S. (2012), *Everyday Spirituality: Social and Spatial Worlds of Enchantment*, Palgrave Macmillan, London.
Mills C. W. (1959), *The Sociological Imagination*, Oxford University Press, New York.
Nesti A. (1985), *Il religioso implicito*, Ianua, Roma.
Nietzsche F. (1881), *Morgenröte. Gedanken über die moralischen Vorurteile*, Schmeitzner, Chemnitz (Eng. Trans. *Daybreak: Thoughts on the Prejudices of Morality*, Cambridge University Press, Cambridge, 1997).
Norris P., Inglehart R. (2004), *Sacred and Secular. Religion and Politics Worldwide*, Cambridge University Press, Cambridge.
Obadia L. (2013), "Désoccidentaliser encore les sciences des religions? La modélisation des 'spiritualités asiatiques' en France et en Europe", in F. Raphaël, A. Piette (coord.), *Revue des Sciences Sociales*, numéro spécial: "Penser le religieux", 49: 122–129.

Palmisano S. (2016), *Exploring New Monastic Communities*, Routledge, Abingdon and New York.
Panikkar R. (1993), *The Cosmotheandric Experience: Emerging Religious Consciousness*, Motilal Banarsidass Publishers, Delhi.
Roof W. C. (1993), *A Generation of Seekers: The Spiritual Journeys of the Baby Boom Generation*, Harper Collins, San Francisco.
Roof W. C. (1999), *Spiritual Marketplace: Baby Boomers and the Remaking of American Religion*, Princeton University Press, Princeton.
Roof W. C. (2003), "Religion and Spirituality: Toward an Integrated Analysis", in M. Dillon (ed.), *Handbook of the Sociology of Religion*, Cambridge University Press, Cambridge: 137–148.
Segalen V. (1973), *Stèles*, Gallimard, Paris.
Simmel G. (1890), *Über soziale Differenzierung. Soziologische und psychologische Untersuchungen*, Duncker & Humblot, Leipzig.
Simmel G. (1992), *Saggi di sociologia della religione*, Borla, Roma (Eng. Trans. *Essays on Religion*, translated by H. J. Helle, L. Nieder, Yale University Press, New Haven, CT, 1997).
Solomon R. (2002), *Spirituality for the Skeptic: The Thoughtful Love of Life*, Oxford University Press, New York.
Spinoza B. (1677), *Ethica ordine geometrico demonstrata*, Rieuwertsz, Amsterdam (It. Trans. *Etica*, Laterza, Roma and Bari, 2009; Eng. Trans. *Ethics*, Penguin, London, 1996).
Stolz J., Könemann J., Schneuwly Purdie M., Englberger T., Krüggeler M. (2015), *Religion et spiritualité à l'ère de l'ego*, Labor et Fides, Genève (Eng. Tr. *(Un)Believing in Modern Society: Religion, Spirituality, and Religious-Secular Competition*, Routledge, Abingdon and New York, 2016).
Turner B. S. (2011), *Religion and Modern Society: Citizenship, Secularisation and the State*, Cambridge University Press, Cambridge.
Untersteiner M. (1967), *Sofisti: frammenti e testimonianze*, La Nuova Italia, Firenze.
Usunier J.-C., Stolz J. (2014), *New Perspectives on the Marketization of Religion and Spirituality*, Ashgate, Farnham.
Vernant J.-P. (1962), *Les origines de la pensée grecque*, Presses Universitaires de France, Paris (Eng. Trans. *The Origins of Greek Thought*, Cornell University Press, New York, 1982).
Vernant J.-P. (1965), *Mythe et pensée chez les Grecs. Études de psychologie historique*, Éditions Maspero, Paris (Eng. Trans. *Myth and Thought Among the Greeks*, Urzone, New York, 2006).
Vernant J.-P. (1985), *La mort dans les yeux. Figures de l'autre en Grèce ancienne*, Hachette, Paris.
Vernant J.-P. (1989), *L'individu, la mort, l'amour. Soi-même et l'autre en Grèce ancienne*, Gallimard, Paris.
Vernant J.-P. (1990), *Mythe et religion en Grèce ancienne*, Seuil, Paris.
Vernant J.-P., Vidal-Naquet P. (1972), *Mythe et tragédie en Grèce ancienne I*, La Découverte, Paris (Eng. Trans. *Myth and Tragedy in Ancient Greece*, Urzone, New York, 1988).
Vernant J.-P., Vidal-Naquet P. (1986), *Mythe et tragédie II*, La Découverte, Paris.

4 Sense of religion in the secular age

What is the significance of defining ours as a *post-secular age*? The preposition *post* in *post-secular* and *post-secularisation* has sometimes assumed a temporal meaning, as in an age which follows upon another, rather than the causal meaning of an age which sees the operation of all the effects of the preceding era. But the significance of this, our religious age following upon a secular (i.e. non-religious) age, is ambiguous because it might indicate that in this era secularisation has ended and there is a return to the *sacrum* as the datum unifying every sector of society. To avoid such ambiguity, this section will use the *secular* concept, more precise than *post-secular*. The first sub-section (*Post-secular* versus *secular*) touches upon the strange phenomenon of the *post-secular* concept among sociologists. The second (*Leaving [behind] the heteronomy of the religious*) indicates the process, beginning in the eighteenth century, of departing from religions on the part of sciences, technology, life in society and the individual's self-understanding. The passage from heteronomy to autonomy means moving on from a destiny which falls upon the individual from outside and from determinism fatal to individual choice. In political terms it indicates the passage from absolute monarchy to democracy; in religious terms, the passage from religion to spirituality. The relationship between heteronomy and autonomy implies an inevitable loss of "natural innocence" and an increase of responsibility. The third sub-section (*The religious beyond the secular*) documents the fact that secularisation, while reducing religious organization in Western European societies, does not contradict the persistence of religious life on a personal scale or sensitivity to questions about individual and collective human destiny. The fourth and last (*Structure of the religious in the future*) points out some homologies in the context of advanced modernity, inevitable parallels between economic, socio-cultural and religious structures.

Post-secular versus *secular*

The metaphorical concept of *post-secular* was introduced by Filippo Barbano and Luigi Berzano in a 1990 work in order to designate the present age, characterized both by *secularisation* as a general social differentiation process and by *post-secularity* as the situation where the effects of secularisation on the social, cultural and religious system are at their greatest and most numerous (Berzano, 1990). *Post-secular* should not be understood to mean that secularisation processes are no longer present but rather that, from a combination of circumstances, they have brought about a situation on the very terrain of disenchantment and secularisation where important cultural phenomena concerning connections between the world – albeit secularised – and the experience, history and knowledge of religion are revealed. The secularisation effect has not emptied religion of its religious experience, its history or its knowledge but has transformed its connections with the diversity of a secularised world. For historical religions the *post-secular* condition is characterized not only by all the effects of secularisation but also by new spiritual opportunities and connections made available by living in secularity. Religious times, spaces, structures and forms continue to exist at the heart of technological society and in the heart of technological humankind (Weber, 1920–21; Wilson, 2016).

This ambivalence of northern hemisphere religiosity was already glimpsed by Max Weber in the introduction to his *Economy and Society*:

> Questions of universal history will inevitably and legitimately be dealt with by the children of the modern European cultural world using this operational approach: what combination of circumstances has brought about the situation that in the West itself, and only there, have cultural manifestations appeared which – at least to the extent that we like to believe – belong to a universal line of development of meaning and validity?
>
> (Weber, 1982: 3 [our translation])

In this sense the *post-secular* concept allows a re-interpretation of some of Weber's own elements of the sociology of religion which do not follow from his theory of secularisation, such as those of "spiritual dispositions" which characterize modern man. These new interests and "spiritual dispositions" – which we shall call *post-secular* – are characterized by their sense of action aimed at re-assembling what differentiation-secularisation dismantles daily in various areas of existence (economic, political, social, ethical and spiritual questions). *Post-secular religiosity* (action, intentionality, the need for identity re-composition) is seen in two main thrusts. The first is a fundamental anthropological condition, what Weber called "a feeling of unprecedented interior loneliness on the part of the individual" connected with the "great historical-religious process of disenchantment of the world which began with ancient Hebrew prophecy and which, aligned with Greek scientific thought, rejected as superstition and impiety all magic means of seeking salvation" (Weber, 1965: 177 [our translation]). The second consists of a multiplicity of situations involving *morality* and *ethics* (genetic engineering, sexuality, illness, environment, ethnic diversity and so on), the *social* context (prevalence of individualistic, egotistical ego), the *political* (separation of morality and politics) and the economic (autonomy of material, consumerist interests) (Giordan, Possamai, 2018).

This original *post-secular* concept contrasts with the ambiguous use made of it, especially after Habermas re-proposed it in 2005 (Habermas and Ratzinger, 2005). The *post-secular* concept – together with that of *post-secularisation* and, recently, *post-axial* – understood as the end of secularisation remains ambiguous and is contradicted by the facts. No research is available to document the return today of the sacred or of God after their recent disappearance. In the cited original meaning, *post-secular* did not indicate leaving behind the *secular* age but rather the transformation of religions within modern/secular social structures and a new sense of the religious on the part of individuals. Considering the generalisation of its use, it would be useful to give up the *post-secularity* metaphor and the adoption of the clearer *secularity* concept.

Interest in researching the religious sense continues in *secular* society: reflecting on one hand the permanence – not only residual – of religion as a cognitive and normative element and, on the other, indicating its transformations in both the public and private spheres. The cognitive task of the research is to analyse its signs and sources in its various dimensions. The first is that of religion which – when immersed in the secularisation flow as a differentiation phenomenon – ends up by having less social relevance in certain sectors. This is one of the material effects of secularisation, which is simply reflecting today's diversity of religious experience. The second dimension is that of religion which increasingly appears as personal experience in relation to the ethical-religious connections of social action, where religion remains with the function of re-assembling what secularisation has fragmented and differentiated between politics and religion, modernity and tradition, Church and State and, finally, between rationality and transcendence.

Leaving (behind) the heteronomy of the religious

An example of the above is the final part of Marcel Gauchet's already-cited *Le désenchantement du monde*, an important case of the *post-secular* effects of secularisation. Even if data from this early-millennium partly contradict Gauchet's theses, they are still relevant. Analysing Christianity's role in the formation of modern man, the French sociologist does not consider the religious-secular relationship as contradictory, locating it in a historical, consequential development and viewing the Christian religion as the "vector" of modernity. If the scientific rationality of modern Western society does not oppose Christianity as its adversary, but rather obtains from it – even activates – its deep principle, then science is not Christianity's *other*.[1] In outlining the structural complicity between Christianity and modernity, Gauchet carries his thesis to its extreme conclusion: modern society represents complete abandonment of religions, but that does not mean that the religious should no longer speak to humankind.

This process of leaving religions behind began in the eighteenth century and continued to evolve with the development of science, technology, life in society and individual self-understanding. Gauchet repeatedly emphasizes that it is a process which regards the structures of historical realities without denying the space of individual religiosity. It is a profoundly important historical process which began with Greek polytheism and continued with Christianity. It is this historical thread which has led humanity to modern Western secularisation, the present age of the "religious without religion".[2]

> Throughout almost all of human history religion has been primarily and fundamentally a means of structuring human-social space, a way-of-being of societies. Its primordial nature is to be a linking organization between men in the light of their dependence upon the invisible or the supernatural. All the rules which hold us together come from outside, from before and above us. The power which we obey represents the otherworldly law among us. Originally religion is the organization of heteronomy.
>
> (Gauchet, 1992: 159 [our translation])

According to Gauchet, religions in the West are by now socially and politically irrelevant because they no longer possess the socially structuring power which characterized them for centuries. The age of religions was when a certain temporal legitimacy reigned. The present age, on the contrary, is based upon "the state's monopolistic appropriation of the social bond" (Gauchet, 2007: 127). Even though in a society believers remain as such, or traces of religiosity or substitutes of the religious experience are formed, this does not prevent society – qua society – from remaining atheist. Gauchet says two mistakes should be avoided: one is to base oneself on the existence of such a subjective nucleus to disinter the permanence or unchanging nature of religion's social function; and the other is deducing, from the undoubted decline of the role of religion in our societies, that it is a certain sign that religion is destined to vanish without trace. Gauchet does not claim to be methodically exploring the anthropological substratum of experience of the invisible, which is discovered by the retreat of the institutional invisible, but limits himself to indicating some premises which could be useful for research aiming to analyse the condition of man *after* the man of religion. Three streams in this map of the "religious after religions" need to be studied: the *undifferentiated*, the *aesthetic experience* and *man as his own problem*.

The first defines the Other as a content of thought. It is the *undifferentiated*, the void or nothingness, extreme images of the unlimited-undifferentiated, the mystical pole which one reaches at the end of research into the unsubstantial substance.

> This largely explains the tendency to adopt the language (especially Buddhist and Taoist) of Oriental spirituality. No theistic implication, no reference to a separate subjectivity: the *void* or *nothingness* which they suggest is therefore in itself more capable of expressing the pure experience of thought whose expression needs to be supplied than are the usual categories of Christian theology.
> (Gauchet 1992: 294–295 [our translation])

Aesthetic experience is the second stream in continuity with what for millennia has been the sense of the sacred. It is our emotional capacity in the face of the sight of things, the imagination of reality. It is the experience of both the gushing closeness of the Other and its essence, its vacuum.

The third stream of experience through which we place ourselves in irreducible continuity with the man of religion is experience of the problem we are for ourselves. After religions man is still a problem for himself. The decline of religions is paid for by the difficulty of being a subject. In the "*après*-religion" condition, each one has to find one's own answers for oneself. This explains the constant fascination with past ways of believing, with encyclopaedias of salvation and calendars of sense. It explains why many "*après*-religion" people feel the need to convert, in whatever direction. And there are always new and better reasons why their conversions are neither firm nor long-lasting. In reality "*après*-religion" people are incapable of giving up the reasons which induce them to convert. "Comings-and-goings and halting compromises between adherence and distance, between the cult of the problem and choosing the solution, define the age's specific religiosity and perhaps the lasting modality of the survival of the religious in a world without religion" (ibid.: 300 [our translation]).

As is clear by now, Gauchet is an "atheist believer" in the West. By writing a religious history of politics, he intended to base rationality on the

Sense of religion in the secular age 67

religious. By deeply historicising the development of rationality, he traces it back to a religious origin. Contrary to all the tradition of thought about "doubtful faith", Gauchet overturns its interpretation in favour of a religion which becomes the precedent cultural apparatus and founder of modern rationality. The socially disappeared religion, which is to say no longer organized and perceived as an institutional structure of *secular* society, remains with people as a personal and community fact of religious forms. In analysing the concept of leaving (behind) the heteronomy of religion, Gauchet's work interests us because of its conclusion dealing with the (including unexpected) effects of secularisation – that is to say, its religious effects. Unfortunately the work breaks off at point where it would have been most interesting, i.e. an analysis of (relatively) absent forms of instituted religion. This is the point where analysis of the sociology of *secular* society is most relevant: analysis of the set of needs, spiritual expectations and practices which secularisation has made partially autonomous from instituted religions.

Secularity determines further forms of secularisation, especially in single individuals' demand for autonomy in their choice of lifestyles. But what is happening functions in such a way that nothing which is secularised disappears but rather assumes the form of an element which has separated from another element: thus the sacred separates from the profane, the civil from the ecclesial, the practical from the functional, the innovative from the traditional, visible religion from the invisible, public religion from the private and so on with other differentiations. On looking closer the reality of new spiritualities is an effect which can be correlated with the emergence of the effects of *religious secularity*, which stimulated alternative socialisation processes opposite to those whose centrality determined secularisation. The main emphasis on secularisation – of which this volume is a part – is also a lexical choice made by researchers, but it does not erase the reality of some facts related to both individual and collective "human inadequacy" when faced with the general sense of life. To share Bauman's conclusion: "I believe that God will die with man, not a moment before" (Bauman, 2011: 147 [our translation]). Except that in this *secular* age, not even new religious fragments or new spiritualities are always traceable to subjectivities whose identification can be univocally determined; this, too, is an effect of the loss of centrality caused by secularisation as differentiation (Kaell, 2017; Possamai, 2018).

The religious beyond the secular

Going beyond the secularisation analysed by scholars from Max Weber onwards, today's secularisation of lifestyles represents a further form of leaving religion. As we have seen, the autonomy of society's religious structure extends to include individual practices, diminishingly deriving from one's religion of belonging and increasingly from personal choices, thereby becoming more problematical and reflexive. It is clear that when we speak about leaving religion we are not referring to individuals' faith but to the organizational model of those societies which no longer adopt religion as their structural basis. These transformations already came about in the paganism of ancient Greece and Rome which preceded Jewish, Christian and Muslim monotheism. The work of Jean-Pierre Vernant, already cited, documents the fact that, when Greek civilisation was at its height, the organization of the world was no longer religious: nobody believed in effective assistance from the Gods and tragedy dealing with religion was only fiction (Vernant, 1990).

The new relationship of religion with public socio-political institutions – which, for the West, was the main event of modernity, and whose influence spread over the whole planet – has by now encouraged a religious feeling mostly perceived as belonging to the individual sphere; to the extent that the modern legal revolution has provided the basis for original individual rights deriving their legitimacy from what today we call "the rights of man". If the divine does not belong to the order of the material and temporal, it must be collocated only in the heart of man and in the transcendence which he perceives in himself. As Blaise Pascal writes in his *Pensées*: "The heart, and not reason, feels God. And this is faith: God sensed by the heart and not by reason" (Pascal, 1670, pensée 278 [our translation]).

The situation in Europe today is that even some Christian believers reformulate their religious beliefs in terms which are compatible with the principle of rejecting heteronomy. In non-secular societies, however, religious heteronomy establishes individual and collective living, so much so that "disobeying legitimate authority is considered as attacking religion itself, criticizing power as blasphemy, lack of respect towards the established order as desecration, calling into question the subject of authority as a rebellious act" (Legros, 2005: 139 [our translation]). Religion as religion is an institutional fact, a human-social fact of heteronomy. This is the perspective of Gauchet who – not by chance – does not write about secularisation but about the "fading of religion as heteronomy" (Gauchet, 1985). But where is this process heading, and what will be its effects, now that in Europe too religions with very different views of laicity, of religious and cultural pluralism and of secularisation/heteronomy are meeting?

The emergence of heteronomy, which is really the disappearance of the religious design of Western European societies, does not contradict (as we have seen) the persistence of religious life on a personal level. Indeed, even in contexts of maximum secularisation – the vanishing of heteronomy – the private dimension of religion, eschatological questions concerning human individual and collective destiny, a sense of basic life experiences and the overall ethical orientation of existence still prevail. Spiritualities and their multiplication of forms belong to this personal realm. One might say that by now religion – from the point of view of leaving heteronomy – is seen only in forms of spiritualities as the location of sense, of answers to questions about the good life and salvation. It is spiritualities that deal with matters of love, death, suffering and all the important existential problems. Spiritualities, which have always been present in all religions – Christianity, Judaism, Islam and (partially) in Buddhism – are today lay spiritualities often linked to the traditions of the great philosophies, bearers of answers to existential questions but without passing through faith in God or historical churches.

According to Gauchet, Christianity was the first driving force which produced religion's leaving of heteronomy. If that were true, it would clarify even more the constitutive principle of secular modernity: the principle of the person. It is the unitary conception of the individual in Christian monotheism itself which subtracts it from the relational structures and networks determining it and, at the same time, instituting it as a single entity.

To conclude: Leaving religion (behind)? Perhaps, but three questions remain open.

First, there are still today two billion Christian faithful in the world. Then there is the two-thousand-year-old history of Christianity: the architectural nobility of the great cathedrals, Michelangelo's domes, the peerless beauty of monasteries, the evocativeness of Romanic churches dotting mediaeval pilgrims' itineraries, the hundreds of thousands of shrines and stone crosses strewn about the countryside in many parts of the Western world. Add to this the music which reaches its highest point with Bach's cantatas and Passions; then sacred painting and literature which still inspire novels and films. In a physical and cultural landscape so distinguished by the history which began with the advent of Christianity, most Europeans still declare themselves to be Christian.

Second, the most politicized religion today is Islam. Its presence as a political force is connected not so much with the failure of modernisation as with some of society's post-political forms, the collapse of the mechanisms which traditionally safeguarded loyalty within the community. Islam does not just show a political face: it is itself politics representing the social fabric. Going far beyond its spiritual dimension, Islam constitutes a space for its affiliates' identities and passions. Even recent forms of fundamentalism are rather a return to politics qua politics than to religion in the political sphere.

Third, the profound relationship established by monotheistic religions between the individual and his/her God, which guaranteed the autonomy of the political organization. What other forms can guarantee the autonomy of the political organization? Is *à la française* laicity not perhaps an exception? Is Christianity not perhaps the only monotheism to have realised, at least partially, the going out from the self in the same historical context in which Islam is the most politicized religion?

Islam's political dimension survives as an essential element even in minor forms, albeit more among Sunnis than among Shias. Khomeini asserted: "The Islamic religion is a political religion; it is a religion in which everything – including devotional gestures and prayer – is politics". The formula that Islam is either politics or nothing indicates that we are not talking about belief but about a force conceived as a political-cultural programme, an instrument and sign of collective identity, a part of public space controlled by the "group of believers" to assert its hegemony. This political dimension of Islam derives from its theological vision where God/Allah does not contain the concept of either real or symbolic paternity. In this "genealogical desert" between God and man, God intervenes only when the paternal function is missing or when structures of relationship and consanguinity have difficulty in taking root. This was Freud's problem with Islam since he had based all his theory of religion on the God/Allah-father correspondence, and on the sense of guilt which unites siblings for having killed their father. The God/Allah-father desert is the place where politics is instituted and the unexpected topicality of Islam activated. The *umma*, the community of Muslim believers, is the superimposition of the religious and the political. The community is directly rooted in the word of God. Furthermore, in the "genealogical desert" the *umma*, egalitarian and revolutionary brotherhood formed out of the void, represents the most alive form of Islam. In reality the most effective affirmation of Islam is where young people find themselves without the traditional protective network of the family and identity with the *umma*. In that situation Islam reveals its propensity to be for its faithful politics, morality, a right – and, above all, an identity.

Structure of the religious in the future

The hypothesis here is that in the future four homologies will operate; inevitable correspondences among economic, socio-cultural and religious structures deriving from the common conditions of advanced modernity independently of the functions these structures will fulfil in various economic, cultural and religious contexts. The effects will include the end of ethnic and ascribed religious identities, independence of religious experience from religious affiliation, living in the midst of pluralism and secularisation and the passage from religions to spiritualities. We already partly know the effect of such homologies on Christianity – but how will they influence other religious worlds?

1. *Weakening of ethnic and ascribed religious identities.* Almost by inertia the traditional grasp of religious identities in the face of accelerating

Sense of religion in the secular age 71

transformations of beliefs, practices and experiences diminishes in all secularised environments. In the past an individual ran up against greater problems and difficulties when s/he abandoned his/her identity/religious belonging *entirely* instead of just giving up some beliefs and practices. The present level of autonomy of religious beliefs, experiences and practices, in addition to ethical-moral convictions, will also cause a transformation of all ethnic-based religious identities. Spiritual fragmentation – until the nineteenth century involving only elite groups in society – recently has spread out through the masses. This phenomenon, which Charles Taylor calls "the nova effect", has transversally affected all social classes (Taylor, 2007). This cannot be fully explained by universal education which brought about a generalisation of the cultural condition previously the preserve of the elite, or by social differentiation which has reduced religion to one of the many separate spheres in the social context, like economics, politics and science. The "nova effect" is part of the global structure of the world which was created in freedom and in the ever-faster multiplication of information, unthinkable without new media, starting from the web.

2. *Independence between religious experience and religious affiliation*. In the secular age traditional forms of the spiritual – and also of the atheistic – are transformed into subjective, experiential and independent forms of the same religious belonging. All this can be seen from the multiplication of spiritualities inside every religion: spiritualities here meaning set of elements, sensibilities, languages, interests, attitudes and community forms particular to specific groups and individuals; spiritualities, in a word, as lifestyles. In the general definition a style concerns the ways in which collectivities make singular the values, rhythms and forms of their life, as well as their ways of being and doing. Thus it refers to systems of perception, representations of meanings and symbolic expressions in evolution. Therefore styles of spiritualities are *not* a fixed, unchanging set of behaviour and symbols reproduced equally from one generation to the next. So we see the general characteristics of secular spiritualities: individualised, experiential, autonomous and in the form of designer spiritualities.[3] Empowerment makes the new spiritualities freer from historical-religious traditions and ecclesiastical organizations, and they cannot avoid following the general movement of deconstruction of whatever is transmitted merely by inertia: religious movements will take the deconstructive path already beaten by literature, music, art and family, educational and political institutions.

3. *Living in pluralism*. Peter L. Berger considers religious pluralism, the condition and "immanent frame" in which all individuals live, to be so important that he prefers the definition "pluralist age" to Charles Taylor's "secular age". Berger (2017: 161 [our translation]) writes: "The expression 'secular age' does not throw light on the empirical state of things which can be seen in most of the contemporary world. The basic proposition which I

assert in this book is rather that it is preferable to define our age as 'pluralist' rather than 'secular'".

Pluralism is not only religious but also scientific. At the dawn of the third millennium, religions can no longer avoid a meeting with the autonomy of science, of politics, of culture, of bio-ethics and individual human rights. No religion can dictate absolute rules forever. The evolution of individual lifestyles in itself, independently of their religious belonging, shows how few affiliates of various religions are able to resist temptation in the end – that of the consumer values embedded in modernisation. Ostentatious consumption, the fascination of appearances and all the other myths of super-modernity challenge believers' styles, whatever religion they belong to. In turn, diaspora situations – where a few believers live among a majority of non-believers – which are common in the secular age, pose for believers the problem of reconciling conscience and behaviour and, consequently, those of their identity and their difference (as individuals and/or groups) from other churches and religions. But with regard to these topics believers arrive on the wave of psychological and social interests typical of advanced modernity, where personal identity-building is the starting-point of practical and theoretical reflection (Berger, 2014).

4. *From religions to spiritualities*. One last point needs to be made about the fact that religions increasingly appear in the form of spiritualities. To frame this phenomenon of spiritualities, it would be useful to indicate the three defining perspectives of religion which, according to scholars, have developed from the nineteenth century onwards (Berzano, 2017; Giordan, 2009; Torpey, 2017).

Religion as neurosis was established as early as the eighteenth century and its history progressed with various visions of religion: in Feuerbach it is interpreted as (among other things) fetishism, in Marx as the opium of the people, in Freud as neurosis and in Nietzsche as nihilism. It is a criticism of religion seen as "fetishism": a – partly imaginary and partly rational – intellectual activity which constructs a product (in this case the idea of God) and then at once forgets that it itself has been the constructor. The principle of this criticism was already contained in Voltaire's famous statement that God created man in his own image and then man did the same thing, creating God in his own image. This definition of religion as superstition, as fetishised hypostasis or as alienation – which perhaps interests us only marginally – is worth considering since much current criticism derives from Voltaire's idea that the divine is simply a human projection. Man made God. Religion is a fetish. It is the commonest and most superficial discourse of atheists.

Religion as heteronomy – which we have seen above – is the political definition of religion in the true sense of the word. Religion is the basis and external source of laws, of the community's social and political organization, and also of individuals' sense of life. According to Marcel Gauchet, the religious is not just heteronomy (i.e. the fact of assigning a different origin to law from humanity itself) but also the negation of human beings' autonomy because it prevents them from attributing social organization, history and the production of laws to themselves (Gauchet, 1985, 1989, 2007). Refusing to perceive humanity as the source of social organization, laws and politics means shifting the source to a transcendent, external, superior power – in short, establishing a fundamental dependence. In Gauchet's most radical view, it is European history which has been the deepest and most structural bond between religion and social organization. For this reason he rejects the terms *secularisation* and *laicisation* because in the past belonging to a religion was not just a superficial belonging to be overtaken today by simply abandoning delusions and superstitions defeated by the Enlightenment of reason and science. Rejecting religion as heteronomy implies overcoming traditional forms of political organization where law is conceived as an inheritance from a tradition which, in its turn, is rooted in an immemorial divine past. This social organization structure, where everything originates "outside", began to weaken after the French Revolution and the birth of a state in which society organizes itself with autonomous laws and regulations.

Religion as spiritualities returns, in secular societies, to what the great ancient philosophies once were: theories and doctrines about the meaning of life, health and salvation which illuminated finiteness, life and death, and the quest for living well. Religion as spirituality is the site of support, of sense, of answers to questions about the good life. Spiritualities, with their function of responding to the individual's existential doubts without going through faith in God, no longer oppose morality to spirituality or philosophy to spirituality. In this their sapiential function we rediscover today Christian, Jewish, Muslim and Buddhist religious spiritualities as well as lay spiritualities without God and linked to the great philosophical traditions. A philosophy analogous to the aims and contexts of today's lay spiritualities can be found at the heart of the Enlightenment, in a passage by Nicolas de Condorcet:

> Our hopes for the destiny of the species can be traced back to these three factors: the abolition of inequality among nations, progress with regard to equality within nations and, finally, true completion of man either by means of improvement in behavioural principles and moral practice or through real refinement of intellectual, moral and physical faculties.
> (Condorcet, 1822: 17 [our translation])

This last form of *religion/spirituality* is the one scholars refer to when they speak about "light wisdom", where health and salvation coincide. In contrast with traditional religious spiritualities based on renunciation, otherworldly ascesis and detachment from the things of this world, the new "light wisdom" guarantees material success, inner harmony, serenity and self-confidence, comfort and ease – in the *here and now*. Everybody can gain access, and an invisible hand guides this new market of goods and spiritual services with great democracy. The mass media, radio and television broadcasts, books, magazines, DVDs and so on all have a determining function. Thanks to the communications revolution it has become possible, for the first time in the history of our planet, to deliver the technical means of "self-fulfilment" to new spiritual consumers. And this is the latest form of transmission of the sacred in modernity.

Notes

1 The same thesis of the liberation of the sacred through secularisation, and as an effect of Christian *kerygma*, is particularly evident in the work of the German theologian Friedrich Gogarten (cf. Gogarten, 1953, 1948, 1968). This is also Dietrich Bonhoeffer's position, even though the Lutheran theologian never uses the term *secularisation* (cf. Bonhoeffer, 2005).
2 The passage from heteronomy to autonomy means passing from a destiny which "falls upon" an individual from outside, and from determinism as destiny, to individual choice. In the political field it means passing from absolute monarchy to democracy, and in the religious from religion to spirituality. In this heteronomy-autonomy relationship, according to Michael Sandel, there is an inevitable loss of "natural innocence" and a growth of responsibility. This is the democratic condition which demands responsibility from everybody (Sandel, 2007).
3 *Designer religion* is the expression used by some sociologists to indicate the individual construction of a religious lifestyle, analogous to what happens in the construction of clothing, musical preference, dietary, sport and free-time lifestyles. Other scholars speak of "tailoring religion to fit one's needs" to interpret individuals' growing trend to seek their own spiritual preferences. See Berzano, 2017.

References

Bauman Z. (2011), *Living on Borrowed Time*, Polity, Cambridge (It. Trans. *Vite che non possiamo permetterci*, Laterza, Roma-Bari).
Berger P. L. (2014), *The Many Altars of Modernity: Toward a Paradigm for Religion in a Pluralist Age*, Walter de Gruyter, Boston and Berlin (It. Trans. *I molti altari della modernità. Le religioni al tempo del pluralismo*, EMI, Bologna, 2017).
Berzano L. (1990), *Differenziazione e religione negli anni Ottanta*, Giappichelli, Torino.
Berzano L. (2017), *Spiritualità. Moltiplicazione delle forme nella società secolare*, Bibliografica, Milano.
Bonhoeffer D. (2005), *Un cristianesimo non religioso*. Antologia da "Resistenza e resa" *e* "Lettere alla fidanzata", EMP, Padova (Eng. Trans. *Letters and Papers From Prison*, Macmillan and Co., London, 1953).
Condorcet M., Caritat J. A. N. (1822), *Esquisse d'un tableau historique des progrès de l'esprit humain*, Masson et Fils, Paris.
Gauchet M. (1985), *Le désenchantement du monde. Une histoire politique de la religion*, Gallimard, Paris (It. Trans. *Il disincanto del mondo: una storia politica della*

religione, Einaudi, Torino, 1992; Eng. Trans. *The Disenchantment of the World: A Political History of Religion*, Princeton University Press, Princeton, NJ, 1997).
Gauchet M. (1989), *La Révolution des droits de l'homme*, Gallimard, Paris.
Gauchet M. (1992), *Il disincanto del mondo: una storia politica della religione*, Einaudi, Torino.
Gauchet M. (2007), *L'avènement de la démocratie, La Révolution moderne* (v.1), *La crise du libéralisme* (v.2), Gallimard, Paris.
Giordan G. (2009), "The Body Between Religion and Spirituality", *Social Compass*, 56, n. 2: 226–236.
Giordan G., Possamai A. (2018), *Sociology of Exorcism in Late Modernity*, Palgrave Macmillan, Cham.
Gogarten F. (1948), *Die Verkündigung Jesu Christi. Grundlagen und Aufgabe*, Schneider, Heidelberg.
Gogarten F. (1953), *Entmythologisierung und Kirche*, Vorwerk-Verlag, Stuttgart.
Gogarten F. (1968), *Die Frage nach Gott: eine Vorlesung*, Mohr Siebeck, Tübingen.
Habermas J., Ratzinger J. (Benedetto XVI) (2005), *Ragione e fede in dialogo*, Marsilio, Venezia. (Eng. Trans. from the Original German edition, *The Dialectics of Secularisation: On Reason and Religion*, Ignatius Press, San Francisco, 2006).
Kaell H. (ed.) (2017), *Everyday Sacred: Religion in Contemporary Quebec*, McGill-Queen's University Press, Montreal and Kingston.
Legros R. (2005), "La naissance de l'individu moderne", in *La naissance de l'individu dans l'art*, Grasset, Paris.
Pascal B. (1670), *Pensées de M. Pascal sur la religion et sur quelques autres sujets [. . .]*, Desprez, Paris (It. Trans. *Pensieri e altri scritti*, Mondadori, Milano, 1987; Eng. Trans. *Pensées*, Penguin, London, 1966).
Possamai A. (2018), *I-zation of Society, Religion, and Neoliberal Post-Secularism*, Palgrave Macmillan, Cham.
Sandel M. J. (2007), *The Case Against Perfection: Ethics in the Age of Genetic Engineering*, Belknap Press of Harvard University Press, Cambridge, MA and London (It. Trans. S. Galli, *Contro la perfezione. L'etica nell'età dell'ingegneria genetica*, V&P, Milano, 2008).
Taylor C. (2007), *A Secular Age*, Harvard University Press, Cambridge, MA.
Torpey J. (2017), *Three Axial Ages: Moral, Material, Mental*, Rutgers University Press, New Brunswick, NJ.
Vernant J.-P. (1990), *Mythe et religion en Grèce ancienne*, Seuil, Paris.
Weber M. (1920–21), *Gesammelte Aufsätze zur Religionssoziologie*, Mohr, Tübingen (Eng. Trans. *The Sociology of Religion*, Methuen, London, 1965).
Weber M. (1965), *L'etica protestante e lo spirito del capitalismo*, Sansoni, Firenze (Original Edition *Die protestantische Ethik und der Geist des Kapitalismus*, Mohr, Tübingen, 1904–05; Eng. Trans. *The Protestant Ethic and the Spirit of Capitalism*, Penguin, London, 2002).
Weber M. (1982), *Sociologia della religione*, Edizioni di Comunità, Milano (Original Edition *Wirtschaft und Gesellschaft*, Mohr, Tübingen, 1922; Eng. Trans. *Economy and Society*, Bedminster Press, New York, 1968).
Wilson B. R., edited by Bruce S. (2016), *Religion in Secular Society: Fifty Years On*, Oxford University Press, Oxford.

Index

1968 18, 21, 23, 26

abstract Logos 3, 31, 35
abstract thought 35
active imagination 21
adfecti tristi 34
advanced modernity 2, 7, 45, 47, 62, 70, 72
aesthetic experience 66
aestheticization of society 10, 11
aesthetics 11–15
aesthetic society 10
agnostic 44
agnosticism 32, 58
aisthesis 12
à la carte religion 20, 47
à la française laicity 69
alienation 50, 72
Altglas, V. 3
Ammerman, N. T. 45
amor fati 34
ana-theist 44
anomic society 27
Ansart, P. 8
anticipatory socialisation 14
Antoninus Pius 38
après-religion 66
Aristotle 12, 31–32, 34–35, 37, 58
atheism 11, 19, 44, 48, 51–52
autonomy: from heteronomy to 62, 74; scientific 30, 39; *see also* lifestyle(s)
autonomy of faith 57
autonomy of science 3
axial age 27

Barbano, F. 63
Baudrillard, J. 10

Bauman, Z. 1, 67
Baumann, M. 45
Beck, U. 1, 45
Becker, H. S. 15
being 11, 23
believing without belonging 44, 53
Bellah, R. 48
belonging *see* communities of belonging; inertia of belonging; religious belonging; types of belonging
belonging without believing 44
Benjamin, W. 12, 51
Berger, B. 15, 24, 40, 55
Berger, P. L. 15, 22, 24, 45, 55, 71–72
Bernard de Clairvaux 51
Berzano, L. 2, 8, 16, 24, 26–27, 49, 53, 56, 63, 72, 74
Bonhoeffer, D. 74
Bourdieu, P. 8
Buddha 27
Buddhism 69

Calasso, R. 42–43
Campiche, R. 45
Canticle of Canticles 51
Carta, G. 14
Cartesian Rationalism 31
Casanova, J. 40
Catholic Church 47–48, 51
Chaos 34
Chicago School 13, 15
choice(s): free 2, 54; personal 7, 54–55, 67; successive 24–25
Christian churches 21, 24
Christian God 38
Christianity 27, 30–31, 33, 35–38, 42, 50–51, 65, 69, 70

Christian message 37
Christian morality 37
Cipriani, R. 45
circular conversions 56
City of Man 31
Classical philosophy 3
collective memory 13
Colledge, R. J. 52–53
communities of belonging 41
Condorcet, M. 73
consumption 6–7, 10–11, 13–15, 18, 26, 28, 72
convergence culture 28
cosmic order 34–36, 38
Cosmos 31, 34–35

D'Agostini, F. 32, 58
Dahrendorf 1
dasein 13
Davie, G. 45, 53
Dawkins, R. 52–53
De Groot, K. 4
Dennet, D. C. 52
Descartes 54; *see also* Cartesian Rationalism
design 10
designer religion 26, 47, 74
designer spirituality 20, 71
Detienne, M. 30, 32
deviancy 15
differentiated subjectivity 24, 46
differentiation 4, 13, 20–21, 23, 25, 39, 46, 56, 63–64, 67, 71
digital spirituality 45
Dilthey, W. 12
dischenchanting/disenchantment 31
disenchantment 19, 30, 39, 43, 52, 63–64
distinction 20
divine-humanity 31, 35, 38
divine substance 42
divinisation of the human 38
DIY religion 20, 47
Dumazedier, J. 14–15
Durkheim, É. 27, 42, 49
dynamis 37

Elias, N. 6
empowerment 13, 47, 71
energeia 37
Englberger, T. 45, 55

Enlightenment 54, 73
Erfahren 12
Erfahrung 12
Erlebnis 12–13
Ethica 34
ethical rupture 36
ethics 12, 64
etsi communitas non daretur 41
etsi deus non daretur 31, 41
Eumenides 32
extra Ecclesiam nulla salus 55

Fabris, G. 14
Ferry, L. 19, 31, 34–35, 38
Feuerbach 72
first secularisation 30, 32
Fokas, E. 45
fourth secularisation 3, 30–31, 41, 43, 45, 48–49, 54
fractal religious forms 42
freedom 1, 3, 31, 34, 37, 43, 47, 50, 57, 71; *see also* religious freedom
French Revolution 73
Freud, S. 50, 70, 72
Frisby, D. 7
Frontisi-Ducroux, F. 30
Fuller, R. C. 48
function sign 10

Garelli, F. 45
Gauchet, M. 4, 19, 54, 64–69, 72–73
Gauthier, F. 45
generative elements 8–9, 53
Genova, C. 2, 8, 27, 47–49, 53, 56
Giddens, A. 1, 7
Gilli, G. A. 39
Giordan, G. 45, 64, 72
God/Allah 70
Godless spirituality 50, 52–53
Gogarten, F. 74
good life 34–37, 69, 73
Gorski, P. S. 3, 45
Greek morality 36
Greek mythology 3, 30, 33
Greek philosophy 19, 31–35, 37–38, 54
Greeks 34, 36–37
grey conformity 3
grey conformism 10
Grotius, H. 31, 41, 51
group *see* IN group; OUT group

groups of reference 14; *see also* reference groups
Guizzardi, G. 45

Habermas, J. 64
habit 8, 11–12, 24
habitus 8
having 23
health 38, 46, 47, 73
Heelas, P. 19
Hegel 11, 54
Hegelian Rationalism 31
Hervieu-Léger, D. 23
Hesiod 32–33
heteronomy 4, 62, 64–65, 67–69, 72–73; *see also* religion as heteronomy
Homer 32–33
homme moyen 43
homo aestheticus 10–11
homo consumericus 15
homo saecularis 43–44
Horace 34
horizontal identity 55
horizontal lifestyles 2, 3, 55
horizontal religion 31
horizontal religiosity 54–56
horizontal society 2, 27, 55
Houtman, D. 24
humanisation of the divine 31, 35, 38
Humanism 31, 36; *see also* modern humanism
humanist secularism 43
humanist secularity 43

ideal type 9
identification 9, 14, 20, 24–25, 48, 54–57; *see also* strong identification
identities 2, 6, 18, 25, 27, 56–57, 69; individual 23, 31, 55; multiple 19; multiple spiritual 25; religious 2, 3, 44, 57, 70–71
identity 8, 13–15, 24–26, 39, 44, 54, 56–57, 63, 70–72; religious 1, 46, 57; spiritual 24–25, 43, 46; *see also* horizontal identity; strong identity, weak identification
identity-building 6, 54, 56–57, 72
identity state 21
immanent transcendence 49
implicit religion 26

individualisation 20, 27, 46
individualism 11, 23, 55; *see also* super-individualism
individuation 20–22; *see also* spiritual individuation
inertia of belonging 43
Inglehart, R. 2–3, 23, 45
IN group 7
Islam 69–70

Jaspers, K. 27
Jedlowski 8, 12
Judaism 69
Jung, C. G. 20–21
Justin 36, 38

Kaell, H. 76
Kant 11, 54
Kellner, H. 15, 24, 55
Khomeini 70
Könemann, J. 45, 55
Krüggeler, M. 45, 55
Kyuman Kim 45

laicisation 73
laicité 43
lay Europe 40
leben 13
Le Bras, G. 1
Legros, R. 68
Lemert, E. M. 15
Leone, M. 44–45
Lerat, C. 45
Lévinas, E. 51
L'Homme-Dieu 35
Liber Novus 21
lifestyle(s): *autonomous* 42; autonomy of 30, 41–45; definition of 7–10, 53; individual 3, 49, 72; multiple 3; multiplication of 13, 46; religious 7, 24–27, 47, 49, 53, 74; secularisation of 3, 31, 67; *see also* horizontal lifestyles
Lifton, R. J. 55
light wisdom 73–74
liturgies 11, 22, 49
Livolsi, M. 15
Logos 30–36, 38; *see also* abstract Logos
Logos-Man 31, 35

loisir(s) 10, 14–15, 57
loving 23
Luckmann, T. 22

MacKian, S. 45
macro-secularisation 40
Man-God 36
Marcus Aurelius 36, 38
Martikainen, T. 45
Mascini, P. 24
Matza, D. 15
Mauss, M. 18
meaning 8–11
Merton, R. K. 14, 16
meso-secularisation 40
micro-secularisation 40
Mills, C. W. 52
modern humanism 54
modernity 3, 11–13, 19, 30–31, 37, 39, 40–41, 44, 48, 50, 52, 64–65, 68, 72, 74; *see also* advanced modernity; super-modernity
morality 3, 11, 33, 40, 47, 54, 64, 70, 73; *see also* Christian morality; Greek morality; Stoic morality
multiple I 46
mythological dome 32
mythos 30–31

natural place 34–35
needs *see* three areas of needs
Nesti, A. 45
New Age 50
New Age religiosity 47
Nietzsche, F. 11, 34, 51, 54, 72
Norris, P. 3, 45
nova effect 71

Obadia, L. 45
objectivisation 22
objectivity of the style 22
Odyssey 33–34
Oresteia 32
OUT group 7

Pace, E. 3, 45, 56
Palmisano, S. 49
Panikkar, R. 52
panta rei 12
Park, R. 24

Parmenides 32
Pascal, B. 68
Passeron, J.-C. 8
Perniola, M. 12
philosophy: death of 36; *see also* Classical philosophy; Greek philosophy; Stoic philosophy
pilgrims of the absolute 44
pivotal age 26
Plato 32, 37, 58
pluralisation 15, 24, 26
pluralisation of the worlds of life 7
pluralism 23, 56, 68, 70; *living in* 71; multiple forms of 26; religious 1, 28, 71
pluralist age 71
Possamai, A. 64, 67
post-axial 64
post-axial religions 27
post-modern 13
post-modernity 11
post-secular 62–64
post-secular age 62
post-secularisation 62
post-secularity 63–64
post-secular religiosity 63
post-secular society 28, 51
practice(s) 1–4, 8–15, 18, 20, 22–23, 25–26, 28, 30–31, 39, 40–43, 47–50, 52–54, 57, 67, 71, 73; *see also* spiritual practices
practising without believing 49
Prina, F. 16
processes of socialisation 15
profane 1, 4, 6, 25–26, 38–39
Protagoras 32–33, 58
protean 55
Protestantism 44

Quack, J. 25

Rationalism *see* Cartesian Rationalism; Hegelian Rationalism
Ratzinger, J. 64
reference groups 10, 14, 16
Reformation 52
re-legere 49
re-ligare 49
religion *see* à *la carte* religion; *après-*religion; *designer religion*; DIY

religion; horizontal religion; implicit religion; post-axial religions; scenery religion
religion as heteronomy 72
religion as neurosis 72
religion as spiritualities 73
religiosity 12, 40, 44, 49, 50–51, 63, 65–66; rebirth of multiple 27; *see also* horizontal religiosity; New Age religiosity; post-secular religiosity
religious affiliation 53, 70–71
religious America 40
religious belonging 11, 24, 26, 71–72
religious beyond the secular 62, 67
religious DIY 47; *see also* DIY religion
religious experience 4, 19, 27, 57, 63–65, 70–71
religious field 3, 10, 18, 22–25, 41–42, 44–46, 49
religious freedom 27, 31, 54
religious market 1, 14, 56
religious patchwork 47
religious secularity 25, 67
religious sense 44–45, 64
religious sphere 48–49, 55
religious subsystem 39
religious without religion 65
Renaissance 52
return of the subject 23–24
revolution of rising (spiritual) expectations 15, 19, 23
Rigal-Cellard, B. 45
rights of man 68
rites of passage 7, 39
rituals 19, 22, 26, 33, 39, 42, 47
Ritzer, G. 15
Rolland, R. 50
Roof, W. C. 21, 23, 47, 48
rupture *see* ethical rupture; spiritual rupture; theological rupture; triple rupture

sacred 1, 3–4, 6, 10, 12, 19, 25–26, 30, 32–33, 39, 45, 52, 64, 66–67, 74
sacred face 50
sacrum 30, 32, 62
saeculum 30, 32
Saint John 36
Saint John's Gospel 36
Saint Paul 36
salvation 27, 34–35, 37–38, 46, 55, 64, 66, 69, 73
Sandel, M. J. 74
SBNR 44
scenery religion 26
Schneuwly Purdie, M. 45, 55
Scholasticism 36
Schuh, C. 25
second secularisation 31, 35, 38
secular age 4, 18, 45–46, 62–74
secular condition 24–25, 42–44
secular context 4, 21
secular forms 19, 43
secular I 52
secularisation 1, 3–4, 11, 23, 25, 30–33, 39–40, 52, 54, 57–58, 62–65, 67–68, 70, 73–74; *see also* first secularisation; fourth secularisation; macro-secularisation; meso-secularisation; micro-secularisation; second secularisation; third secularisation
secularisation process 4, 24, 32, 40, 42, 63
secularism 58; *see also* humanist secularism
secularity 24–25, 58, 64, 67; *see also* humanist secularity; post-secularity; religious secularity
secular phase 19
secular sacred 4
secular sensibility 11
secular society 18, 39, 42, 50, 52, 64, 67
Segalen, V. 51
self-fulfilment 23–24, 74
sense 8
serial relations 55
serial relationship 57
Sheilaism 48
silent revolution 3, 23
Simmel, G. 3, 6–8, 11–13, 22, 46, 50
situational geography 7
social action 8, 64
social cohesion 39, 42, 47
social form(s) 2–4, 8, 13, 45, 48
social worlds 24–25, 46
society *see* aestheticization of society; aesthetic society; anomic society;

Index 81

horizontal society; post-secular society; secular society; traditional society
sociological horizontality 54
Socrates 27, 58
Solomon, R. 52
Sophists 32–33, 58
Spinoza, B. 34
spiritual dispositions 63
spiritual happenings 45
spiritual I 24, 52
spiritual individualisation 20
spiritual individuation 19, 20, 22
spiritualities 20–22, 28, 40–43, 46, 49–50, 52–53, 69–73; multiplication of 18, 20, 45, 71; new 12, 19, 20–23, 25, 40, 49, 50–51, 67, 71; secular 26, 46, 71; traditional 21, 51
spirituality 11–12, 20–22, 24, 28, 38, 46, 51; *see also* designer spirituality; digital spirituality; *Godless spirituality*
spiritual practices 22–23, 43
spiritual provisions 25
spiritual revolution 18–19
spiritual rupture 37
spiritual sensibility 24, 53
spiritual transformations 26
spiritual voyage 20
status symbols 49
Stoic(s) 31–32, 35–38
Stoic God 38
Stoicism 34
Stoic morality 36
Stoic philosophy 35, 38
Stolz, J. 3, 5, 45, 48, 55
strong identification 56
strong identity, weak identification 56
style(s) 3, 6–8, 10–11, 13–15, 18, 21–23, 25, 27, 41, 45, 47–49, 54, 56, 71–72; *see also* objectivity of the style
style of life 3, 6–8, 10, 21; *see also* lifestyle(s)
style symbols 49
style to *styles* 21–22
stylistic personalisation 24

subsystem(s) 39–40
super-individualism 47
super-modernity 72
Sutherland, E. H. 16
symbolic interactionism 15

Taylor, C. 23, 71
Theion 31, 34–36, 38
Theogony 32–33
theologians 55
theological rupture 35–36
third secularisation 3, 31, 36, 39, 41
three areas of needs 23
Torpey, J. 45, 72
traditional society 6, 10, 21, 23, 39, 46
transcendence 12, 18, 22, 44–45, 51–52, 64, 68; *see also* immanent transcendence
transcendency 53
triple rupture 35
Turner, B. 45
types of belonging 24

Ulysses 34–35, 37
umma 70
uncertainty 1, 7, 40, 44
undifferentiated 66
Untersteiner 32
urbanisation of consciousness 55
Usunier, J.-C. 48

VanAntwerpen 45
Vatican Council II 21
Vernant, J.-P. 30, 32–33, 68
vertical reproduction 1, 3, 10, 27
Vidal-Naquet, P. 30
Voltaire 72

weak links 56
Weber, M. 3, 8–9, 18–19, 30–31, 39, 41, 43, 51–52, 63–64, 67
wellbeing 43, 46
Wilson, B. R. 63
Wirth, L. 13
Woodhead, L. 19
Works and Days 32
Wuthnow, R. 23

For Product Safety Concerns and Information please contact our EU representative GPSR@taylorandfrancis.com
Taylor & Francis Verlag GmbH, Kaufingerstraße 24, 80331 München, Germany